VARIETY

by

Paul Valéry
of the French Academy

Translated by
MALCOLM COWLEY

New York
Harcourt, Brace and Company

CONTENTS

ACKNOWLEDGMENT

Thanks are due The New Republic *for permission to use as the Introduction to this volume the essay which appeared in its issue of December 8, 1926, under the title, "Toward a Universal Man."*

INTRODUCTION

Shortly after his twentieth birthday, Paul
Valéry came to Paris. It was during the autumn
of 1892, when the Symbolist movement was at its
height, and when poets were struggling desperately
and diversely to renew the vigour of French verse.
"More fervour, courage, and learning," he says,
"more researches into theory, more disputes, and a
more pious attention have rarely been devoted, in
so short a time, to the problem of pure beauty."
Into these struggles Valéry entered; a few of his
poems were published in the Symbolist reviews;
and Mallarmé, the leader of the movement, became his close friend.

His early poems attracted the attention of the
few people who have the power of making and
unmaking literary reputations. A brilliant career
was predicted for him. However, since a literary
career in France has its own conditions and aims,
I had better stop to give a definition. The poet
who will later be successful begins by experiment

and rebellion. People are shocked by his boldness, then commence to enjoy it. Slowly a public is formed for his work, and reacts on the poet by insensible degrees; it makes him more conservative or conservatively daring; it restricts his aims to writing and being praised. To make his public larger, he attempts a novel. He begins to aspire to the Academy, makes propitiatory visits to its members, and finally, at the age of sixty, he is elected, becoming a member of the official hierarchy, officially immortal. His financial success may be relatively small—equal only to that of third-rate British or American authors—but in point of fame, his rewards are infinitely greater than theirs. . . . Such was the consecrated road, with enough difficulties to make the journey interesting, which stretched in front of Valéry; and such was the goal from which he turned aside, only to reach it incidentally, in his pursuit of more permanent honours.

I am not trying to sketch his biography, something which demands a different treatment. I am only attempting to explain the significance of a very remarkable career; and in this career the most important event was his ceasing to write, in order

to devote himself to more essential aims. Imagine
the situation. A young man who has conceived
the ideal of pure poetry, and in some of his poems
has approached this ultimate goal, turns slowly
aside from what had been his interests. He studies,
seeks for a fundamental attitude underlying all
the operations of the mind, and tries to develop his
own mind as an instrument of precision. All his
values, and not his alone, are transformed. And
when he begins once more to write for publication,
after a silence of twenty years, literature no longer
exists for him as an end in itself or a means of
earning praise; it is simply a form of mental exercise, to be valued because it is difficult. His
primary object is a defence of the conscious mind.

It was in 1917 that Valéry published *La Jeune
Parque,* and other poems followed in fairly rapid
succession. Each was limited to an edition of a
thousand copies or less. The literary world, however, was beginning to speak of him once more;
and in answering one of those questionnaires to
which French magazines turn when they can think
of nothing else to fill their pages, the French poets
named him as the most distinguished of their number. The choice caused some sensation, for Valéry

was still unknown to the great public; and he so remained, in great part, till his election to the Academy. The place he was given was that of Anatole France—a curious comment on the changing literary ideals of two generations.

Since then he has undergone something like an apotheosis. It began with the publication of *Variety*, the first of his books to appear in a popular edition. This volume of essays had an astonishing circulation; my own copy of the French text belongs to the twenty-fifth printing, and others have since been made. Critics and more critics expounded his ideas; I should estimate that over a hundred times as much has been written about Valéry as he himself has written. He is compared to Baudelaire and Racine, to Pascal, Bossuet, Descartes, Montaigne; indeed, to almost every French writer of genius. In other countries, Germany and Italy most of all, his works are widely read, explained, translated; and his reputation has spread over all the Continent. I don't know how many times I have heard him described as the greatest (or the only great) contemporary writer. Meanwhile he remains unchanged: thinking a great deal, writing a little, publishing after long delays, and compromising with his public not in the least.

I met him in 1923, and we talked about his work. Having forgotten his exact words, I shall have to be content with repeating the notes I made the following day, while the conversation still was fresh in my mind. "He writes poems," I observed, "as a laboratory experiment in thought. He obeys the conventions of verse as if they were the rules of a game he chose to play. He would not violate the laws of chess or tennis and substitute new laws of his own. . . . People tell him, 'You write in a certain manner; therefore you are a classicist.' Not in the least; he is simply a person. His poems exist independently of this person, and are not necessarily an expression of himself. . . . He has experimented all his life. Now, after the classical and perfect verses he has lately published, if he should write something 'modern,' his admirers would be surprised; but such a change would be in no way alien to his nature."

These notes will help to explain some of the opinions he advances in his essays. As for the essays themselves, they deal with themes which were none of his choosing; he accepted the assigned subjects in the spirit of the game. At this point, fortunately, I can quote from the prefatory remarks:

"Each of these essays . . . is the result of a circumstance; the author wrote none of them spontaneously. Their subjects were not of his choice; even their length was sometimes *given*. Almost always surprised, at the beginning of his work, by finding himself involved in an unaccustomed order of ideas . . . he was obliged, each time, to recover the natural direction of his thought. All the unity of this *Variety* resides in that one gesture."

Three observations on what this note implies: The first is that these alien, these *given* subjects serve better than deliberately chosen themes to show the operations of a mind which is a magnificent instrument. Valéry is not alone in possessing an "instrumental" mind. In civilizations which have reached the stage of ours, there are numbers of men who can solve any problem set them, but cannot set themselves problems. They lack direction. Independence they also lack, for their careers, their personalities, even, are determined by outside influences—the books they are asked to write, the formulæ they are asked to discover, the portraits they are commissioned to paint, or the trades to which they are apprenticed. If the objects set them are unworthy, their minds deteriorate, and in a period of idleness will rust as quickly as a piece of delicate machinery left standing in the rain. . . . But Valéry alone has discovered a solution: that is, he has recovered his independence by making the instrumentality of his mind an end in itself; by seeking continually to protect and develop that instrument.

The second observation is that the "natural direction of his thought," which he tries to recover, has led him in most cases to transform the subject completely. Always he seeks to carry his ideas to their limit; to discover something "more intense or exact than the given object." As a result his titles are too modest. "Adonis," for example—an essay in which he sets out to deal with an early poem of La Fontaine—is soon transformed into a general defence of the laws of verse. His "Tribute" to Marcel Proust is a discussion of the novel under its broadest conditions; and often in his essays on Pascal and Poe's *Eureka* he gropes toward a statement of our fundamental attitudes to the universe.

Finally we can say that, for Valéry's readers, the

unity of this *Variety* is more fundamental than the author concedes. It resides in the essential unity of his thought, whatever the subjects on which that thought is exercised. From the two introductory letters, which are a general summary of his attitude, to the profound analysis of Leonardo da Vinci with which the volume closes, everything is directed toward a defence of the intellect, of the conscious mind. It has need of defenders in our time. Against Freudianism, for example; not in its legitimate applications, but in its literary aspects, where it results in the notion that poems are comparable in every respect with dreams. Against the super-realists. Against that school of writers led by Anderson and Lawrence which counsels drift and surrender to our instincts. Against the metaphysics of behaviourism. Against the sociological theory of art—that it is determined entirely by social and economic factors: add x to y and Shakespeare is the result. Against determinisms in general. Against Spengler's idea that, ours being a declining civilization, we have nothing left but to sail ships and make ourselves millionaires. . . . I may be mistaken in grouping these diverse theories, attitudes, and cults, but it seems to me that they represent a pretty general attack on the freedom of the intellect; and they lead us to believe that our culture, the creation of the European mind, has suddenly turned against its own creator.

But among all the enemies of conscious thought, it is specialization which is the most paralyzing. It results in the idea that a real gulf exists between the different activities of the mind: as, for example, between the arts and the sciences. By confining even the great talents to one side or the other of this gulf, it limits the progress in both fields of endeavour. Moreover a specialization, any specialization, becomes a fixed idea, which is a form of hypnosis. And it leads, says Valéry, to a confusion between "the patient observer, the meticulous accountant of existence . . . and the man for whom this labour is performed, the poet of the hypothesis, the builder with analytical materials. To the first, patience, monotonous direction, specialization, and all time. The absence of thought is his quality. But the second must circulate through barriers and partitions. His rôle is to overstep them. . . . Nine times out of ten, every great improvement in a field of endeavour is obtained by the introduction of methods and notions which were unforeseen."

In his magnificent essay on the method of Leonardo, he searches for "the central attitude from which all the enterprises of learning or science and all the operations of art are equally possible." He analyzes the mind of a man who discovered this central attitude. Technically the portrait is one of Leonardo, a man of the Renaissance. Actually it is an ideal to be pursued by our own generation—and one toward which we have been slowly progressing during the twenty years since this essay was first published. The sciences, instead of being further complicated, are becoming simplified through the discovery of central principles; physics is merging into chemistry and chemistry into biology; the artists are studying the conclusions of physicists, mathematicians, psychologists; and it is not impossible that a new Leonardo will arise to include the whole field of intellectual activity in his scope—leaving his theories to guide the methods of every science, and his works as a model for every art.

The universal man . . . This is the ideal which Valéry has given our generation, and it explains why his essays are held in such respect. It also explains why they are read so widely, in spite of his being a rather difficult author. The same remark applies to him which he made of Montaigne and Bossuet: "They do not fear the reader; they measure neither his labour nor their own." And this reader, like Valéry himself, will be surprised by "finding himself involved in an unaccustomed order of ideas, and suddenly placed in an unexpected state of mind."

"But read on," I can imagine some one saying, "read carefully, and you will find a new attitude, both to the world and to the mind, which creates the world in its own image. Read to discover a new manner of regarding the arts and sciences, to find another standard of judgment, and to form ideals for the future which are based not on vague hopes of progress or artistic fulfilment, but laboriously, dangerously, on the lessons of the past."

M. C.

October 15, 1926.

NOTE

Each of these essays which you perhaps will read is the result of a circumstance; the author wrote none of them spontaneously. Their subjects were not of his choice; even their length was sometimes given.

Almost always surprised, at the beginning of his work, by finding himself involved in an unaccustomed order of ideas, and suddenly placed in an unexpected state of mind, he was obliged, each time, to recover the natural direction of his thought. All the unity of this Variety resides in that one gesture.

THE INTELLECTUAL CRISIS

Two Letters [1]

[1] These two letters, written for translation into English, were published in April and May, 1919, by the London *Athenæum*. The present
translation has been made specially for this volume.

THE INTELLECTUAL CRISIS

First Letter

WE modern civilizations have learned to recognize that we are mortal like the others.
We had heard tell of whole worlds vanished, of
empires foundered with all their men and all
their engines, sunk to the inexplorable depths of
the centuries with their gods and laws, their
academies and their pure and applied sciences,
their grammars, dictionaries, classics, romantics,
symbolists, their critics and the critics of their
critics. We knew that all the apparent earth is
made of ashes, and that ashes have a meaning. We
perceived, through the misty bulk of history, the
phantoms of huge vessels once laden with riches
and learning. We could not count them. But
these wrecks, after all, were no concern of ours.

Elam, Nineveh, Babylon were vague and splendid names; the total ruin of these worlds, for us,
meant as little as did their existence. But *France,
England, Russia* . . . these names, too, are splen-

did. *Lusitania* is a lovely name. And now we see that the abyss of history is deep enough to bury all the world. We feel that a civilization is fragile as a life. The circumstances which will send the works of Keats and the works of Baudelaire to join those of Menander are not at all inconceivable; they are found in the daily papers.

Nor is this all. The painful lesson is still more complete. It was not enough that our generation should learn by its own experience how the loveliest things and the most ancient, the most fearful and the best designed, are perishable *by accident*; we have also seen, in the realms of thought, sentiment, and common sense, the appearance of extraordinary phenomena, the sudden realization of paradoxes, the brutal contradiction of probability.

I will cite only one example: The great virtues of the German nation have caused more evils than idleness ever fostered vices. With our own eyes we have seen conscientious labour, the most solid learning, strict discipline, and a worthy diligence, applied to fearful ends.

Without so many virtues, so many horrors would have been impossible. A great deal of science was

4

doubtless required to kill so many men, destroy so much property, annihilate so many cities in so short a time; but *moral qualities* were equally required. Knowledge and Duty: must we suspect you also?

And so the spiritual Persepolis is no less ravaged than the material Susa. All is not lost, but everything has felt itself perish.

An extraordinary shudder has lately passed through the marrow of Europe. It perceived, in all its thinking substance, that it recognized itself no longer, was ceasing to resemble itself, and soon would lose consciousness—a consciousness which it owed to centuries of bearable misfortunes, thousands of first-rate men, and innumerable chances— geographical, racial, historical.

Then, as if for a desperate defence of its physiological self and riches, all its memories returned confusedly. Its great men and its great books reappeared pell-mell. Never did people read so much or with so great passion as during the war; ask the booksellers. Never did people pray so much or so profoundly; ask the priests. All the saviours were invoked; all the founders, protectors, martyrs, and heroes; the fathers of every fatherland, the sainted heroines, the national poets. . . .

And, in the same mental disorder, at the summons of the same anguish, cultivated Europe experienced the rapid revival of its innumerable creeds: dogmas, philosophies, heterogeneous ideals, the three hundred ways of explaining the world, the thousand and one nuances of Christianity, the two dozen positivisms; while the whole spectrum of intellectual light displayed its incompatible colours, casting a strange contradictory glow on the agony of the European soul. Inventors were feverishly searching their imagination and the annals of former wars, in hope of finding a way to remove barbed wire, baffle the submarines, or paralyze the flight of aeroplanes; the soul, meanwhile, was invoking all its known incantations— gravely considering any prophecy, however bizarre; seeking for auguries, refuge, consolations, through the whole gamut of memories, anterior acts and ancestral attitudes. All these are the known products of anxiety; they are the disordered enterprises of the brain which flees from reality to a nightmare and from nightmare to the real, maddened like a rat in a trap.

The military crisis perhaps is over. The economic crisis is visible in all its force; but the intellectual crisis—which is more subtle, and by its very nature assumes the most deceptive appearances, since it takes place in the very realm of dissimulation—this crisis is difficult to grasp in its true point, its phase.

No one can say what will be living tomorrow and what will be dead, in literature, in philosophy, in æsthetics. No one yet knows the ideas and modes of expression which will be inscribed on the list of losses, and the discoveries which will be proclaimed.

Hope, indeed, remains, and sings in a muffled voice:

> *Et cum vorandi vicerit libidinem*
> *Late triumphet imperator spiritus.*

But hope is only man's distrust for whatever his mind foresees exactly. It suggests that every conclusion unfavourable to oneself must be an error of the mind. The facts, however, are plain and merciless: There are the thousands of young writers and young artists who have been killed. There are the lost illusion of a European culture and the demonstrated inability of knowledge to save anything whatsoever; there is science, touched mortally in its ethical ambitions and as if dishonoured by the cruelty of its applications; there is idealism, barely the victor, deeply bruised, responsible for its dreams; realism disappointed, beaten, loaded with crimes and faults; greed and renunciation equally flouted; creeds mingled in both the camps, Cross against Cross, Crescent against Crescent; there are the sceptics themselves, confounded by events so sudden, violent, troubling, that they play with our thoughts like a cat with a mouse—the sceptics lose their doubts, find them again, lose them, and cease to be the masters of their thoughts.

The ship has pitched and tossed too long; the stoutest lamps are finally overturned.

The intellectual crisis is particularly grave and profound because of the state in which it found the patient.

I have neither time nor capacity to define the intellectual state of Europe in 1914. And who would be bold enough to trace a picture of that state? The subject is tremendous; it demands knowledge of every variety and an infinite mass of information. Moreover, when one is dealing with such a complex subject, the difficulty of reconstructing the past, even the most recent past, is in every way comparable with that of constructing the future, even the most immediate; or rather it is the same difficulty. The prophet and the historian are in the same boat; let us leave them there.

At present all I require is a vague and general recollection of what people were thinking on the eve of the war; the researches they were making, the books they published. If, then, I omit all detail, limiting myself to a rapid impression, and to the *natural whole* which is derived from an instantaneous perception, I can see—*nothing!* Nothing—although that nothing was infinitely rich.

The physicists tell us that if our eye could subsist in an oven heated to the point of incandescence, it would see—nothing. No luminous inequality would remain to distinguish the points of space. The result of confining this enormous energy is invisibility, a nonperceptible equality. Now, an equality of this nature is nothing else than *disorder* in its perfect state.

And in what consisted the disorder of our mental Europe? In the free co-existence, in all cultivated minds, of the most dissimilar ideas, the most contradictory principles of life and knowledge. That is precisely what characterizes a *modern* epoch.

I have no objection to generalizing the notion of "modern," and applying this name to a certain mode of existence, instead of making it a mere synonym of "contemporary." There are moments and places in history where we can introduce ourselves, *we moderns*, without greatly troubling the harmony of those times, without being infinitely strange or conspicuous against their background; without appearing as clashing, dissonant, unassimilable beings. Wherever our entry would be least sensational, there we are almost at home. It is clear that the Rome of Trajan and the Alexandria of the Ptolemies would absorb us more easily than many places less remote in time, but more specialized in a single type of customs, and entirely devoted to one race, one culture, and one system of life.

Well, the Europe of 1914 had perhaps reached the limit of this modernism. Every brain of a certain rank was a focus for every nationality of opinion; every thinker was a World's Fair of thoughts. There were works of the mind so rich in contrasts and contradictory impulses that they made one think of the absurd lighting effects which distinguished the capitals of those days; the eyes were dazzled and grew weary. . . . How many materials, how many labours, calculations, and plundered centuries, how many heterogeneous lives added together were needed to furnish the background for this carnival; to enthrone it as form of supreme wisdom and triumph of humanity?

In one book of that period, and by no means the most mediocre, it is no effort to detect the influence of the Russian ballet—a little of Pascal's sombre style—many impressions of the Goncourt type—something of Nietzsche—something of Rimbaud—certain effects due to converse with painters, and sometimes the tone of scientific monographs—the whole perfumed with a vaguely British spirit which is difficult to define! . . . Let us remark in passing that each of the components of this mixture contained many other *bodies*. To seek for them is useless: it would be repeating what

I just said about modernism, and cataloguing all
the mental history of Europe.

Today, on an immense platform which might be
that of Elsinore, but runs instead from Basle to
Cologne, touching the sands of Nieuport, the
marshes of the Somme, the granites of Alsace, and
the chalky plateaus of Champagne—the European
Hamlet stares at millions of ghosts.

But he is an intellectual Hamlet. He meditates
on the life and death of truths. For phantoms he
has all the subjects of our controversies; for regrets
he has all our titles to glory; he bows under the
weight of discoveries and learning, unable to renounce and unable to resume this limitless activity.
He reflects on the boredom of recommencing the
past, on the folly of always striving to be original.
He wavers between one abyss and the other, for
two dangers still threaten the world: order and
disorder.

If he takes a skull in his hands, the skull is illustrious.—"Whose was it?"—That was *Leonardo*.
He invented the flying man, but the flying man
has hardly fulfilled the purpose of the inventor;
we know that the flying man mounted on his great

swan (*il grande uccello sopra del dosso del suo magno cecero*) has other uses in our days than to go fetch snow from the mountain-tops and sprinkle it over city streets in the heat of summer. . . . And this other skull is that of *Leibnitz,* who dreamed of universal peace. And this was *Kant, Kant who begat Hegel, who begat Marx, who begat* . . .

Hamlet hardly knows what to do with all these skulls. But if he throws them away! . . . Will he then cease to be himself? His fearfully lucid mind surveys the passage from war to peace. This transition is more dangerous, more obscure than the passage from peace to war; all nations are convulsed by it. "And I, the European intellect, what will become of me? . . . And what is peace?" he asks. "*Peace is perhaps the state of things in which the natural hostility of man toward man is manifested by creation, in place of the destruction which marks a war.* It is the period of creative competition and the struggle of inventions. But as for me, am I not weary of inventing? Have I not exhausted the desire for extreme attempts and made a vice of my skilful fabrications? Must I abandon my difficult duties and my transcendent ambitions? Should I follow the movement like Polonius, who has become the editor of a great newspaper? like Laertes, who is somewhere in the aviation? like Rosenkrantz, who does I don't know what under a Russian name?

"Phantoms, farewell! The world has no more need of you. Nor of me. The world, which has given the name of 'progress' to its tendency toward a fatal precision, is seeking to unite the blessings of life with the advantages of death. A certain confusion still reigns, but yet a little while and all will be made clear; at last we shall behold the miracle of a strictly animal society, a perfect and final ant-hill."

Second Letter

Peace, I was saying the other day, is that form of war which admits acts of love and creation; hence, it is something more complex and obscure than war in the strict sense, just as life is more profound and more obscure than death.

But the beginning and setting in motion of peace are more obscure than peace itself, just as fecundation and the origin of life are more mysterious than the functioning of the being which has already been made and adapted.

Of this mystery, every one is conscious today; it is a sensation physically present. There are doubtless a few men who can perceive their own selves as forming an actual part of this mystery; and perhaps there is some one whose sensibility is clear, fine, and rich enough to examine itself, and there find future phases of our destiny.

Such is not my ambition. The affairs of the world interest me only as they relate to the intellect—everything in relation to the intellect. Bacon would call this intellect an *idol*. I agree, but have found none better.

Hence, when I think of the establishment of peace, it is from the standpoint of the intellect and the things of the intellect. This point of view is *false*, since it separates the mind from all other activities; but this abstraction and falsification are inevitable; every point of view is false.

A first thought appears. Our idea of culture, of intelligence, of masterpieces stands in a very ancient relation—so ancient as rarely to be perceived—with the idea of Europe.

Other parts of the world have had admirable civilizations, poets of the first rank, constructors, and even scientists. But no other part of the world has possessed that extraordinary *physical* property which consists in the most intense power of *radiation* combined with the most intense power of *absorption*.

Everything came to Europe, and from Europe everything has come. Or almost everything.

Now, the present situation permits of this capital question: Will Europe retain its leadership in all activities?

Will Europe become *what she is in reality*: that is, a little cape of the Asiatic continent?

Or will Europe remain *what she seems to be*: that is, the most precious part of the terrestrial universe, the pearl of the globe, the brain of a vast body?

In order to set forth this alternative in all its rigour, I will take the liberty of developing a sort of fundamental theorem.

Consider a map which shows the whole of the habitable world. This whole is divided into regions, and in each of these regions there is a certain density of population, a certain quality of men. To each of these regions also corresponds a natural wealth—a more or less fertile soil, a more or less precious subsoil, a more or less watered territory, more or less adapted to transportation, etc. These characteristics enable us to classify these regions at any epoch, in such a way that at any epoch *the state of the living world can be defined by a system of inequalities between the inhabited regions of its surface.*

At any moment the *history* of the following moment depends on this given inequality.

Let us now examine, not this theoretical classification, but the classification which existed in reality, and still existed yesterday. We perceive a fact which is both remarkable in itself and extremely familiar to us: The little region of Europe stands at the head of the classification, and so has stood for centuries. In spite of its small area, and although the wealth of the soil is not extraordinary, it dominates the picture. By what miracle? Certainly the miracle must reside in the quality of its population. This quality must compensate for the smaller number of men, square miles, and tons of ore assigned to Europe. Put the Empire of

India in one scale of a balance; put the United Kingdom in the other. See: the balance inclines toward the scale with the lighter weight!

Here is an extraordinary upset of equilibrium. But its consequences are more extraordinary still: *they lead us to foresee a progressive change in the opposite direction*.

We suggested a moment ago that the quality of its men must determine the pre-eminence of Europe. I cannot analyze this quality in detail, but I find by rapid examination that burning desire, ardent and disinterested curiosity, a happy blend of imagination and logical precision, a scepticism that is not pessimistic and a mysticism that is not resigned . . . are the more specifically active qualities of the European psyche.

A single example of this European spirit—it is an example of the first rank and of paramount importance. Greece—for all the shores of the Mediterranean belong in Europe, Smyrna and Alexandria being as European as Athens or Marseilles—Greece invented geometry. It was a foolhardy enterprise; we are still disputing over the *possibility* of such folly.

18

In order to achieve this fantastic creation, what had to be done? Remember that neither the Egyptians nor the Chinese, the Chaldeans nor the Hindus ventured so far. Reflect that it was an enthralling adventure, a conquest a thousand times more precious and positively more poetic than that of the Golden Fleece. No mere sheepskin is worth the proposition of Pythagoras.

Geometry was an enterprise demanding gifts which are generally incompatible. It required Argonauts of the mind, hardy pilots who would let themselves neither be lost in their thoughts, nor distracted by their impressions. Neither the fragility of the premises which bore them on, nor the subtlety or infinity of the inferences which they were exploring, could divert them from their course. They were equidistant from the variable negroes and the indefinite yogis. They adjusted common speech to precise reasoning, an extraordinarily delicate and improbable achievement. They analyzed motor and visual operations of great complexity. They made these operations correspond to grammatical and linguistic properties. Blind seers, they trusted in speech to guide them through space. . . . And space itself, as the centuries passed, became an always richer and more surprising creation; it developed along with thought, which was acquiring more mastery over itself and placing more confidence both in the power of reason and in the initial subtlety which had provided it with such incomparable tools: definitions, axioms, lemmata, theorems, problems, porisms, and the rest.

I should need a whole book to discuss the subject. I only wished to specify, in a few words, one of the characteristic acts of the European genius. This very example carries me back to my original thesis.

I was arguing that the inequality which has so long been observed to favour Europe might, *by its own effects*, be changed progressively into an opposite sort of inequality. This is what I called by the ambitious name of a fundamental theorem.

How can we demonstrate this proposition?—I will take the same example, that of Greek geometry, and ask the reader to consider the effects of this discipline through the ages. Little by little, very slowly but very surely, one can see it assuming such authority that all researches and all acquired experience tend irresistibly to borrow its rigorous manner, its scrupulous economy of "matter," its automatic generalization, its subtle methods, and that infinite prudence which permits it the wildest daring. . . . Modern science was born from this education in the grand style.

But once it was born, once tried and rewarded by its practical applications, our science, becoming a means of power, a means of concrete domination, a stimulant of wealth, a device for exploiting the capital of the planet, ceased to be an artistic activity, and an end in itself; instead it has become an exchange value. The utility of knowledge makes it a *commodity,* desired no longer by a few distinguished enthusiasts, but by Everyman.

This commodity, as a result, will be prepared in more and more convenient or comestible forms; it will be distributed to a larger and larger circle of buyers; it will be transformed into something commercial, something which is imitated and produced almost everywhere.

Result: the inequality which used to exist between the different regions of the world, in respect to the mechanical arts, applied sciences, and scientific methods of war or peace—the inequality on which European predominance was based—tends gradually to disappear.

Hence, *the classification of the habitable regions of the world tends to become such that brute size, numbers, and statistical elements—population, area, raw materials—will at last exclusively determine this classification of the compartments of the world.*

And hence, the balance which inclined to our side, although we *seemed* lighter, is slowly beginning to change its direction—as if we had stupidly taken the invisible weight which bore us down and cast it into the other scale. *We have been fools enough to make forces proportional to masses.*

This phenomenon of our times might be compared with another, which can be observed in the heart of every nation; it consists in the diffusion of culture, and in the accession to culture of larger and larger categories of individuals.

To predict the consequences of this diffusion, and determine whether it will necessarily produce a degradation, would be attempting a delightfully complicated problem of intellectual physics.

For the speculative mind the charm of this problem arises first from its resemblance to the physical fact of diffusion, and thence from the sudden change of this resemblance into a profound difference, as soon as the thinker returns to his first subject, which was *men* and not *molecules.*

A drop of wine will fall into water and hardly colour it; after a rosy mist the wine tends to disappear. This is the physical fact. But now suppose that some time after this disappearance and this return to limpidity, we saw drops of *pure wine* being formed here and there in this vessel which seemed once more to contain only *pure water—* our wonder would have no bounds. . . .

This miracle of Cana is not impossible in the field of intellectual and social physics. We then speak of *genius* and oppose it to diffusion.

A short time ago we were considering a curious balance, which moved contrary to weight. Now we are watching a liquid system which passes, as if spontaneously, from homogeneous to heterogeneous, from a thorough mixture to complete separation. . . . These paradoxical images give the simplest and most practical representation of the rôle

23

played in the world by what has been called—for five or ten thousand years—the Mind.

"But can the European mind, or at least its most precious elements, be totally diffused? The exploitation of the globe, the equalization of techniques, democracy—these phenomena point to a *deminutio capitis*, a loss of rights, by Europe; should they be taken as irrevocable decisions of destiny? Or have we some liberty *against* this menacing conspiracy of things?"

It is perhaps by seeking this liberty that one creates it. However, for such a research, we must temporarily abandon the consideration of groups, and study the struggle of personal life against social life in the thinking individual.[2]

---

[2] The continuation and conclusion of this study have not yet appeared. However, many of the ideas in these two letters are further developed in the Note which follows.

NOTE

From an address delivered at the University of Zürich, November 15, 1922.

NOTE

THE storm has died away, and still we are rest-
less, uneasy, as if the storm were about to
break. Almost all the affairs of men remain in a
terrible uncertainty. We think of what has disappeared, we are almost destroyed by what has
been destroyed; we do not know what will be born,
and we fear the future, not without reason. We
hope vaguely, we dread precisely; our fears are infinitely more precise than our hopes; we confess
that the charm of life is behind us, abundance is
behind us, but doubt and disorder are in us and
with us. There is no thinking man, however
shrewd or learned he may be, who can hope to
dominate this anxiety, to escape from this impression of darkness, to measure the probable duration
of this period when the vital relations of humanity
are disturbed profoundly.

We are a very unfortunate generation, whose lot
has been to see the moment of our passage through
life coincide with the arrival of great and terrify-

ing events, the echo of which will resound through all our lives.

One can say that all the fundamentals of our world have been affected by the war, or more exactly, by the circumstances of the war; something deeper has been worn away than the renewable parts of the machine. You know how greatly the general economic situation has been disturbed, and the polity of states, and the very life of the individual; you are familiar with the universal discomfort, hesitation, apprehension. *But among all these injured things is the Mind.* The Mind has indeed been cruelly wounded; its complaint is heard in the hearts of intellectual men; it passes a mournful judgment on itself. It doubts itself profoundly.

What is this Mind? In what respects can it be touched, injured, diminished, humiliated by the present state of the world? Why are intellectual matters in such a miserable state, and whence comes the distress, the anguish, of intellectual men? These are the topics I now propose to discuss.

Man is the separate animal, the curious living creature that is opposed to all others and rises above all others by his . . . *dreams!*—by the intensity, succession, and diversity of his *dreams!*—by their extraordinary effects, which may sometimes even modify his nature, and not his nature only, but that surrounding nature which he tirelessly endeavours to subjugate to his dreams.

I mean to say that man is incessantly and necessarily opposed to *whatever is* by his concern for *what is not!* and that he creates laboriously, or perhaps by genius, whatever is needed to give his dreams the power and precision of reality, and, on the other hand, to force upon this reality the increasing changes which make it resemble his dreams.

Other living creatures are moved and transformed only by exterior variations. They adapt themselves, which is to say that they deform themselves, in order to preserve the essential characteristics of their existence, and in this manner they effect an equilibrium with their environment.

It is not their habit, so far as I know, to break this equilibrium spontaneously. If they are adapted to a certain climate, they do not leave it without some motive, without exterior pressure or necessity. They seek blindly after their own sufficient good, but they do not feel the goad of that *better* which is the enemy of the "good enough," and heartens us to face the worst.

Man, however, has that within him which will break the equilibrium he maintained with his environment. He has that which will render him discontented with everything which satisfied him formerly. At every instant he is something else than he is. He does not form a *closed system* of needs and gratifications for his needs. From such gratification he derives I do not know what excess of power, which destroys his content. Hardly are his body and his appetites appeased when something stirs within him; it torments him, informs him, commands him, goads him on; it directs him secretly. And that something is the Mind, the Mind armed with all its inexhaustible questions. . . .

Eternally it asks within us: Who, what, where, at what time, why, how, by what means? It contrasts the past with the present, the future with the past, the possible with the real, the image with the fact. It is both what precedes and what comes last, what constructs and what destroys, what goes by chance and what proceeds by plan. Thus, it might be called that which is not, and the instrument of that which is not. Finally and principally it is the mysterious author of the dreams I described.

What are the dreams that man has made? . . . Which of these dreams have become reality, and how did they become reality?

Look within us and look about us. Think of the city, or turn the pages of some book at random; or better yet, observe the most instinctive movements of our hearts. . . .

We wish for, we are pleased to imagine, many strange things. These wishes are very ancient, and it seems that man will never resolve not to make them. . . . Read Genesis once more. On the threshold of the sacred book, in the midst of the first steps in the first garden, there appear the dreams of Knowledge and of Immortality; by these fair fruits of the tree of life and the tree of the knowledge of good and evil we have always been tempted. A few pages further, you will find in the same Bible the dream of a completely unified humanity, working together to build a prodigious tower. "And the whole earth was of one language, and of one speech." We dream of this today.

There you will also find the strange story of the

prophet who, being swallowed by a great fish, was able to move in the depths of the sea. . . .

Among the Greeks, there are heroes who construct flying-machines. Others can tame wild beasts. Their miraculous words move mountains, cause the stones to walk and temples to spring into being, all by a sort of marvellous telemechanics.

To act on distant objects; to make gold; to transmute metals; to vanquish death and predict the future; to move freely in spheres forbidden to our species; to speak, see, hear from one end of the world to the other; to visit the stars; to realize perpetual motion—we have dreamed so many dreams that the list would be infinite. But all these dreams together form a strange *programme*, the pursuit of which is in some way attached to the very history of mankind.

In this programme all projects of universal conquest and universal dominion, whether material or spiritual, have their place. Everything which we call *civilization*, *progress*, *science*, *art*, *culture*, relates to this extraordinary creation and depends on it directly. One might say that all these dreams struggle to surmount all the given conditions of our definite existence. *We are a zoölogical species*

*which tends to broaden and diversify its own field
of existence;* and one could form a table, a systematic classification of our dreams, by considering
each of them as directed against one of the initial
conditions of our life. There are dreams against
gravity and dreams against the laws of motion.
There are dreams against space and dreams against
time. Omnipresence, prophecy, and the Fountain
of Youth: all these were dreamed of, and still are
dreamed of under scientific names.

There are dreams against Mayer's principle, and
others against Carnot's principle. There are
dreams against physiological laws and dreams
against the laws and data of ethnology: the equality
of races belongs to the latter class, as does the dream
of eternal and universal peace. . . . Let us suppose that we have drawn up this table and are about
to consider it. We should be quickly tempted to
complete it by the list of realizations. Opposite
each dream we should place whatever has been done
to make it a fact. If, for example, we have placed
the desire to fly in one column, along with the
name of Icarus, then, in the column of acquisitions,
we should inscribe the famous names of Leonardo
da Vinci, Ader, Wright, and their successors. I

might easily multiply these examples; it would be a sort of game which we lack the time to play. Moreover, it would also be necessary to construct a table of disappointments, of dreams which have never been realized. A few of these have been finally condemned: the squaring of the circle, for example, and the gratuitous creation of energy. The others still exist in our not unreasonable hopes.

However, we must return to our table of realizations; this is the one to which I wished to call your attention.

If we consider this very honourable list, we can make the following remark:

Of all these realizations, the most numerous, the most surprising, the most fertile, have been achieved by a fairly limited portion of mankind, in a territory which is very small in relation to the whole mass of habitable lands.

Europe was this privileged place; the European, the European mind, was the author of these marvels.

And what indeed is this Europe? It is a sort of cape of the old continent, an occidental appendage of Asia. By force of nature it looks toward the West. On the south it borders an illustrious sea, the rôle of which (I ought to say the function) has been wonderfully effective in the elaboration of that European mind which is our subject. All the peoples who came to its shores were intermingled; they exchanged blows and merchandise; they founded ports and colonies where not only the objects of ordinary commerce, but beliefs, languages, customs and technical acquisitions were the basis of trade. Even before modern Europe had taken the appearance with which we are familiar, the Mediterranean had seen a sort of pre-Europe established in its eastern basin. Egypt and Phœnicia were in some sort a prefiguration of the civilization which we have fixed; afterwards came the Greeks, the Romans, the Arabs, the Iberian peoples. Around this sparkling water, rich in salt, one imagines a throng of gods and men, the most imposing in the world. Horus, Isis, and Osiris; Astarte and the Samothracian deities; Pallas, Poseidon, Minerva, Neptune, and their like, all reign concurrently over this sea which tossed the strange thoughts of St. Paul, just as it cradled the plans and dreams of Bonaparte. . . .

To these shores, however, where so many peoples had already mingled and jostled and learned from one another, there came in the course of ages still other peoples, drawn toward the splendour of Mediterranean skies, by the beauty and particular intensity of life beneath the sun. The Celts, the Slavs, the Teutonic peoples, all have felt the enchantment of this noblest of seas; a sort of invincible tropism, acting throughout the centuries, has made this admirably formed basin the object of universal desire and the scene of the greatest human activity. Economic, intellectual, and political activity, religious activity, artistic activity, all centre, or at least all seem to originate, on the shores of the inland sea. There it is that one is able to watch the phenomena which preceded the formation of Europe, and to observe, at a certain time, the division of humanity into two groups which grow more and more unlike. The first, which occupies the larger part of the globe, remains in some sort fixed in its customs, learning, and effective power; it no longer progresses, or progresses only by imperceptible degrees.

The other is driven ahead by a perpetual disquiet, a perpetual seeking. The manners and matters of exchange are multiplied; the most varied problems are discussed in its midst; the means of living, of knowing, of self-improvement are accumulated from century to century with astonishing rapidity. Soon the difference in power and practical knowledge between Europe and the rest of the world becomes so great that all equilibrium is destroyed. Europe suddenly bursts its own bounds; it sets out to conquer the world. Modern civilization renews the primitive invasions, but reverses their direction. And Europe, on its own territory, attains the maximum of life, of intellectual fertility, of riches and ambition.

This triumphant Europe which arose from the exchange of all spiritual and material things, from the voluntary and involuntary co-operation of races, from the rivalry of systems, interests, and religions *in a very limited territory*, is bustling and animated; it is a sort of marketplace where all precious things are brought, compared, discussed, and all change hands. It is a stock exchange where doctrines, ideas, discoveries, and dogmas of every nature are *registered*, are *quoted*, rise and fall—becoming the object of the blindest enthusiasm and the most pitiless criticism. Soon imports from the most distant lands are arriving abundantly in this market. On the one hand, the new countries of

America, Oceania, or Africa, and the ancient empires of the East, send their raw materials to Europe to subject them to the astonishing transformations which Europe alone can accomplish. On the other hand, the knowledges, religions, and philosophies of ancient Asia are brought to nourish the ever-wakeful minds which Europe produces in each generation; and this powerful machine transforms the more or less foreign conceptions of the Orient, tests their depth, and extracts their serviceable elements.

Our Europe, which began as a Mediterranean market, thus became a vast factory—a factory in the strict sense, a mill for converting products, but at the same time an incomparable intellectual factory. This intellectual factory receives all the things of the mind from every part of the world, and distributes them to its innumerable machines. Of these, some seize upon every novelty with hope and avidity, exaggerating its value; others employ the brilliance and solidity of the riches already accumulated to resist every innovation. Between acquisition and conservation a dynamic equilibrium must continually be established; but meanwhile an ever more active critical spirit is attacking one tendency or the other, examining without pity the ideas which are favoured or which hold the field, testing and discussing without pity the tendencies of the adjustment which is always obtained.

Our thought must develop, and our thought must be conserved. It advances only by the extremes, but only by the means does it subsist. Extreme order, which is automatism, would be its ruin; extreme disorder would bring it still more rapidly to the abyss.

Finally, little by little, this Europe takes the shape of a gigantic city, with its museums, gardens, and studios, its salons and its laboratories. Here is its Venice; here its Oxford; here are Rome and Paris and Seville. Here are cities which exist for art, or for science, and others which combine ornaments and instruments. This Europe is small enough to be traversed in a time which is very short, and soon will be insignificant. It is large enough to contain all climates, and sufficiently varied to present cultures and landscapes of every nature. From the physical point of view, it is a masterpiece of moderation, of the conjuncture of all conditions favourable to man. And here man has become the European.

I must apologize for giving the words Europe and European a meaning which is a little more than geographical and a little more than historical, but is in some sort *functional*. I might almost say, my thought deforming my speech, that a *Europe* is a kind of system originally formed by a certain human diversity and a particularly favourable locality, and finally moulded by a singularly eventful and living history. The product of this conjuncture of circumstances is a European.

We must examine this character in relation to more simple types of humanity. He is a kind of monster. His memory is too carefully nourished and charged with too many facts. He has extravagant ambitions. He thirsts for knowledge and illimitable riches. Since he generally belongs to a nation which has dominated the world in its hour, and still dreams of its Cæsar, or Charles V., or Bonaparte, there is a pride in him, a hope, and regrets which are always ready to waken. Since he belongs to an age and a continent which have seen so many astounding inventions, so many successful adventures in every field, there is no enterprise, no scientific conquest of which he cannot dream. He is caught between boundless hopes and glorious memories; and if sometimes he happens to fall into pessimism, he thinks in spite of himself that pessimism has produced a few works of the first order. Instead of plunging into mental annihilation, he draws an elegy from his despair. Sometimes, from the same source, he derives a hard and formidable will, a paradoxical motive for actions, based on his contempt for life and humankind.

But who, then, is European?

Here, with many reserves, with the infinite scruples one should have when attempting provisorily to specify something which is not susceptible of real precision, I will risk an essay at definition. What I wish to develop is not a logical definition, but a manner of seeing, a point of view—it being understood that many others exist which are neither more nor less legitimate.

Well, I shall consider all nations as European which, in the course of history, underwent the three influences of which I am going to speak.

The first is that of Rome. Wherever the Roman

Empire held sway, wherever its power made itself
felt, and, in a sense, wherever the Empire was the
object of fear, envy, or admiration; wherever the
nations felt the weight of the Roman sword;
wherever the majesty of the laws and institutions,
the pomp and dignity of the magistrature, were
recognized, copied, sometimes even bizarrely aped
—there something European can be said to exist.
Rome is the eternal model of organized and stable
might.

I do not know the reasons for this great triumph;
it is useless to seek them now, as it is idle to ask
what Europe would have been had it never been
Roman.

But we are concerned only with the fact of the
astonishingly durable imprint left on so many
races, so many generations, by this power—both
superstitious and rational; curiously impregnated
with the judicial spirit, the military spirit, the religious spirit, the spirit of formalism; unquestion-
ably the first to impose the benefits of tolerance
and good administration on conquered peoples.

Then came Christianity. You know how it
spread, little by little, through the whole extent
of the Roman conquest. If we except the New

42

World, which was not so much Christianized as peopled by Christians; if we except Russia, the larger part of which was ignorant both of Roman law and the empire of Cæsar, we perceive that the bounds of the Christian church coincide almost exactly, even today, with the former limits of imperial authority. These two conquests, although so different in their nature, bear a sort of resemblance to each other, and this resemblance is important. The policy of the Romans, which became more ingenious and more supple as the central authority declined in power; that is to say, as the Empire grew in extent and heterogeneity, was responsible for a remarkable innovation in the system of the domination of peoples by one people.

Just as the *city par excellence* ended by adopting all beliefs; by naturalizing all faiths, even the most diverse, and all gods, even the most distant and bizarre—in the same way the imperial government, conscious of the prestige which attached to the name of Roman, did not fear to confer the freedom of the Roman city, the privileges and titles of *civis romanus*, on men of every language and every race. Thus, by the existence of the same Rome, gods ceased to be attached to a tribe, a locality, a mountain, or a city, and became universal, in some sort common to all; while, on the other hand, race, language, and the quality of victor or vanquished, of conqueror or conquered, developed into a uniform legal and political condition which was inaccessible to none. The emperor himself might be a Gaul, a Sarmatian, a Syrian, and he might sacrifice to very foreign gods. . . . It was an extraordinary political innovation.

But Christianity also, in accordance with the vision of St. Peter, and although it was one of the very rare religions which were in ill repute at Rome—Christianity, issuing from the Jewish people, spread through the Gentiles of every race; by means of baptism it conferred on them the new dignity of Christian, just as Rome conferred the Roman citizenship on its former enemies. Little by little it spread through the breadth of the Latin power, and assumed the forms of the empire—*civitas* in the fifth century was the name of an episcopal city. It borrowed everything it could from Rome, and fixed its capital there, not at Jerusalem. It adopted Latin as its language. A citizen of Bordeaux could be a Roman citizen, even a magistrate, and at the same time could be a bishop of the new religion. And the same *Gaul* who was an imperial prefect wrote fine hymns in pure *Latin* to glorify the Son of God, who was born a *Jew* and subject to Herod. Here already is an almost perfect European. A common law, a common God; the same law and the same God; a sole judge for time, a sole Judge for eternity.

The Roman conquest had seized only the political man; its control over minds was only through their exterior habitudes. The Christian conquest, however, aimed at and progressively attained the depths of the moral consciousness.

I shall not even try to measure the extraordinary modifications which the religion of Christ imposed on this consciousness. Even the attempt to explain how radically this faith affected the formation of the European is beyond my design. I am forced to move only on the surface of things, and besides, the effects of Christianity are well known.

I shall mention only a few characteristics of its action; and first, Christianity introduced a *subjective* morality, and above all it imposed the unification of morality. This new unity being placed beside the judicial unity created by the Roman law, analysis, on one side and the other, tended to unify the two codes.

Let us go further.

The new religion required that men examine their own hearts. It was in this fashion that occidentals became familiar with that interior life which the Hindus had been practicing in their manner for centuries; the mystics of Alexandria had also, in their manner, recognized, felt, and deepened it.

Christianity proposes the subtlest, the most important, and even the most fertile problems to the mind. Whether the question is one of the value of evidence, the criticism of texts and sources, or the guarantees of knowledge; whether the problems deal with the distinction between reason and faith, with the opposition which develops between them, and with the antagonism of faith and acts and works; whether we reflect on liberty, servitude, or grace; on spiritual and material powers and their mutual conflict; on the equality of men, the condition of women . . . what more need I add?— Christianity has educated and stimulated millions of minds; has made them act and react during a chain of centuries.

Still we are not perfect Europeans. Something is lacking in our picture; there is lacking that marvellous modification to which we owe not the idea of public order, the cult of the world-city, and the sense of temporal justice; and not the depth of our souls, absolute ideality, and the faith in justice to eternity; but there is lacking that subtle and powerful action to which we owe the best of our intelligence and the delicate solidity of our knowledge—just as we owe the definiteness, purity, and *distinction* of our arts and literature to the same source; it is from Greece that these virtues come.

This time, again, we must admire the rôle of the Roman empire. It conquered to be conquered. Penetrated by Greece, penetrated by Christianity, it offered them both an immense field, organized and pacified; it prepared the site and fashioned the mould into which Greek thought and the Christian idea were later to flow and be so curiously welded.

Our debt to Greece is perhaps what distinguishes us most profoundly from the rest of humanity. To her we owe the discipline of the mind, and the extraordinary example of perfection in all fields of activity. We owe her a method of thinking which tends to relate all things to man, to the complete man; he becomes the *system of references* by which all things must finally be measured. Hence he must develop all the parts of his being and maintain them in a harmony as clear, and even as apparent, as is possible. He must develop his body and his mind. As for the mind, he will defend himself from its excesses, its reveries, its vague and purely fantastic productions, by a detailed criticism and analysis of its judgments, by a rational division of its functions, and by the regulation of forms.

Out of this discipline, science was to originate —our science, which is to say the most characteristic product, the most certain and most personal glory of our mind. Europe is first of all the creator of science. There have been arts of all countries; there has been no true science save that of Europe.

Beyond a doubt, a sort of science existed before Greece, in Egypt and Chaldea, and certain of its results may still appear remarkable. This, however, was an *impure* science, sometimes confused with the technique of one trade or another, and at other times permitting of extremely unscientific preoccupations. Observation has always existed. The reason has always been employed. But these essential elements have little value, and do not obtain a regular success, unless no other factors intervene to corrupt their use.

To construct our science, it was necessary that a relatively perfect model be proposed; that a first masterpiece be offered as an ideal presenting all the precisions, all the guarantees, all the beauties, all the solidities, and defining once for all the very concept of *science* as a pure construction separated from all other aims than those of the edifice itself.

Greek geometry was this incorruptible model; not only the model offered to every science which aims at its perfection, but also an incomparable model of the most typical qualities of the European intellect. I never think of classical art without inevitably choosing the monument of Greek geometry as its best example. The construction of this monument demanded all the rarest qualities, and those which ordinarily are most incompatible. The men who built it were hard and penetrating workers, profound thinkers, but also sensitive artists with an exquisite sense of perfection.

Think of the subtlety and force of will which were required of them before they could accomplish such a delicate, such an *improbable* adjustment of common speech to precise reasoning; think how they analyzed extremely complex mechanical and visual operations, and how well they succeeded in making these operations correspond with the properties of speech and grammar. They trusted to words and their combinations to conduct them surely through space. It is true that this space has become a plurality of spaces and has been singularly enriched; it is true that this geometry, which once seemed so perfect, has allowed many flaws to appear in its crystal. We have examined so closely that wherever the Greeks saw one axiom, we count a dozen. For each of the postulates they introduced, we know that we can substitute several others, and thus obtain a coherent geometry which is sometimes physically applicable.

But think what a novelty was this almost solemn form, so pure and lovely in its general design. Think of this magnificent division of the moments of the Mind, of this marvellous order where every act of the reason is separately placed and clearly

divided from the others; it calls to mind the structure of a temple, that static mechanism whose
every element is visible and declares its function.

The eye considers the load, the support of the
load, the parts of the load, the bulk and how it is
balanced; the eye divides and arranges without effort the orderly masses whose very shape and
vigour are appropriate to their rôle and volume.
These columns, capitals, architraves; these entabla-
tures with their subdivisions, and the ornaments
deduced therefrom without ever exceeding the
limits of their place and harmony, all remind me
of those organs of pure science as the Greeks conceived it: definitions, axioms, lemmata, theorems,
corollaries, porisms, problems . . . that is, the
machinery of the mind made visible, the architecture of the intelligence completely designed—the
temple erected to Space by Speech, but a temple
which can be heightened to infinity.

Such, I believe, are the three essential conditions
which seem to define a true European, a man in
whom the European mind can reside in its fullness. Wherever the names of Cæsar, Gaius, Trajan, and Virgil; of Moses and St. Paul; of Aristotle,

Plato, and Euclid have possessed a simultaneous meaning and authority, there Europe is. Every race and every land which has been successively Romanized, Christianized, and subjected in intellectual matters to the discipline of the Greeks, is absolutely European.

Some countries have received only one or two of these imprints.

There is, then, some trait quite distinct from race, nationality, or even language, which unites and renders similiar the countries of Western and Central Europe. The number of notions and manners of thought which are common to all is much larger than the number of notions which we have in common with a Chinese or an Arab.

I might sum up by saying that there is a region of the world which, in regard to its population, is radically distinguished from all the others. In the realms of power and exact knowledge, the weight of Europe today is still far greater than that of the rest of the world. I am wrong; it is not Europe which excels, but the European mind, of which America is an imposing creation.

Wherever the European spirit dominates, one finds the maximum of *needs*, the maximum of *work,* the maximum of *capital,* the maximum of *returns,* the maximum of *ambition,* the maximum *power,* the maximum *modification of exterior nature,* the maximum of *exchanges* and *relations.*

This collection of maxima is Europe, or the image of Europe.

On the other hand, the conditions of this formation, and of this astonishing inequality, depend evidently on the quality of the individual, the mean quality of *homo europaeus.* And it is remarkable that the man of Europe is not defined by race, or by language, or by customs, but only by desires and the amplitude of his will. . . .

ADONIS

ADONIS

THERE clings to the name of La Fontaine a rumour of day-dreams and idleness, a general murmur of vacancy and perpetual distraction, which naturally suggests the idea of some fabulous creature, always infinitely ready to let himself drift along the gentle current of his life. We see him vaguely, framed in one of those inner pictures which are never far from our thoughts, although it is many years since they took shape, and although they were formed from the first stories and illustration that we knew.

Perhaps, from our earliest childhood, this mere name of La Fontaine, "the fountain," has permanently clothed the imaginary figure of a poet with a vaguely ambiguous sense of depth and coolness, and with no one knows what magic borrowed from living waters. A similiarity in names will often give rise to a myth. From a pun, which is a species of adultery, great gods were sometimes born.

There is, in any case, some one who dreams and

lets himself naïvely drift through life. We tend to place him in a park, or in some enchanting landscape where he seeks the lovely shadows. We give him the spellbound attitude of a hermit who is never really alone; perhaps because he exults with himself at the peace which surrounds him; perhaps because he gossips with the ant, with Reynard the Fox, or with some other of those animals which flourished under Louis XIV. and spoke in such pure French.

If the beasts of the field abandon him—for even the wisest are fickle and easily upset—he turns toward the valleys basking in the sun, where he listens to the voices of the reeds, the nymphs, the mill. He lends them his silence, from which they make a sort of symphony.

He is faithful only to all the delights of the day, but they must give themselves freely; he will not pursue or retain them by force; and one might say that his destiny is content to spin the sweets of every moment into silken threads, and fragilely weave them into infinite hours.

To such a dreamer, nothing is likened more easily than the idle cloud in which his glance confides; to watch it softly drifting across the skies diverts him insensibly from wife and child and self; he forgets his duties as it bears him on; he is freed from all consequences, excused from all fore-thought. For what could be vainer than wishing to outrun the breeze which carries us—unless, perhaps, always to claim responsibility for the movements of a mist?

But a poem of six hundred verses with regular rhymes, like his *Adonis;* such a long succession of graces; a thousand difficulties overcome, and a thousand delights so caught in the length of an inviolable web that they touch and are forced to melt into one another, giving the final illusion of a vast and varied tapestry; all this hidden labour which the lover of poetry considers, as it were, by holding the tapestry against the light, seeking what lies beneath its artifices, turned aside from his search neither by the movement of the hunt nor the vicissitudes of love, and beginning by degrees to admire as his mind succeeds in reconstructing the poet's skill—all this makes him renounce forever the first and primitive idea which he had formed of La Fontaine.

Let us no longer believe that some mere amateur

of gardens, a man who loses his garters like his time; partly inspired and partly addle-pated; a bit silly, a bit waggish, a bit sententious; dispensing a justice based on proverbs to the little beasts which surround him—that such a man could be the real author of *Adonis*. Take heed that the carelessness, here, is studied; the indolence is deliberate; the ease is the height of art. As for naïvety, it must be ruled out of the question; I am convinced that an art and purity so well sustained exclude all thought of idleness or good-natured simplicity.

A simple heart is no equipment for a politician, but neither are dreams and distractions the tools with which words are combined into such rare and precious shapes. The true condition of a true poet is absolutely distinct from the state of dream. In the former I can see nothing but voluntary researches, a struggle to render his thoughts more flexible, and the perpetual triumph of sacrifice.

The man, even, who tries to describe his dream must be infinitely awake. If you wish to imitate, with some degree of exactness, the grotesque inconsistencies of the weak dreamer which you lately

were; through the depths of your mind to pursue
this pensive fall of the soul like a dead leaf through
the vague immensity of memory, do not hope to
succeed without an extreme concentration, which
will lead to your discovering that which exists only
at the price of such concentration.

Whoever says exactitude and style is invoking
the opposite of dream; and whoever encounters
these in a work of art should infer that its author
expended all the time and labour which are necessary to prevent the permanent dissipation of ideas.
The fairest, like the others, all are shadows; and the
kingdom of ghosts, in this case, precedes the kingdom of the living. It was never a mere pastime
to snatch a little grace, or clarity, or permanence
from the confused flow of images, nor to change
the transient into the enduring. And the more
timid, the more fugitive is one's prey, the more
concentration and force of will are needed to render it eternally present, in its eternally fleeting attitude.

Even a fabulist is far from resembling that negli-
gent creature we were pleased in our negligence to
imagine. Phædrus is all elegance; the La Fontaine

of the *Fables* is full of artifice. It was not enough to lie under a tree and listen to the magpie's chatter or the shadowy laughter of the raven; something more was needed to make them speak so gracefully. For there is a strange abyss between the speech of birds or foliage or ideas as it comes to us, and the same speech as we set it down; the interval is beyond conception.

The mysterious difference which exists between even the clearest impression or invention and its finished expression becomes the greatest possible— and hence the most remarkable—when the author subjects his diction to the laws of regular verse. This is a convention which has been very little understood. I will discuss it briefly.

Liberty is such a seductive goddess; she is so particularly seductive to poets; she lays hold of their imagination by dint of such plausible and generally such solid reasons; she is clothed so demurely with novelty and wisdom, and, while hiding their drawbacks, she tempts us with so many advantages to abandon the ancient rules, to consider their absurdities, to reduce them to merely observing the natural laws of the soul and the sense of hearing, that

one hardly knows at first what to answer. Can
one even suggest that this charmer is a dangerous
ally of carelessness, when she can so easily show us
an overwhelming quantity of very bad, very facile,
and terribly regular verses? It is true that an equal
quantity of irregular verses are just as detestable.
This accusation flies back and forth between the
two camps; the best soldiers of one party are the
weaklings of the other; and these weaklings so resemble each other that it is impossible to say why
they should be divided.

Hence, even if a choice were absolutely necessary, it would be difficult to make. As for me, I
think that both sides are right, and every one must
do as he sees fit. But I cannot help being fascinated by the obstinate fashion in which the poets
of all times, down to the days of my youth, loaded
themselves with voluntary chains. It is difficult
to explain why this servitude was hardly perceived
for centuries, and then was found unbearable.
What is the reason for this immemorial obedience
to commandments which seem to us so futile?
Why should the greatest men, whose success depended so much on giving the highest degree of
liberty to their minds, persist so long in an error?

Will it be necessary to solve this enigma by a paradox, as the fashion has been since the decay of logic, and to think that we have an *instinct* for the *artificial?* The two words are utterly incongruous.

Another thing surprises me. Our epoch has seen the birth of almost as many prosodies as poets, or rather a few more systems than individuals, for some individuals brought forth several systems. However, during the same period, industry and the sciences were pursuing the opposite policy. They created uniform measures. They adopted units and standards the use of which was prescribed by laws and treaties; whereas every poet, taking his own nature for a collection of modules, was trying to establish his own body, the personal period of his rhythm, and the duration of his breath as absolute types. Each made a universal diapason of his ear, a universal chronometer of his heart.

In this way poets were running the risk of being poorly understood, poorly read, poorly declaimed; or at least of being understood in a fashion they never expected. This risk is always very great. I should not say that a misinterpretation is always to our disadvantage, nor that a curved mirror never lends us beauty. However, those who dread the uncertainty of communication between writers and readers will certainly find that the fixed metres and more or less artificial symmetries of traditional verse have the advantage of limiting this risk very simply—let us say, if you wish, very coarsely.

As for the tyranny of these rules, it is no greater, in itself, than the tyranny of language, syntax, or vocabulary.

I might carry the apology a little further. I do not think it impossible to give this convention and these so contestable rules a singular value of their own. To write regular verses doubtless involves one's submission to an alien law, rather absurd, always harsh, and sometimes barbarously cruel; this law destroys an infinite number of fine possibilities, but at the same time it suggests a multitude of distant and totally unexpected thoughts. (As for the latter, I shall admit that half of them were not worth the trouble of being born, and that the other half, on the contrary, bring us enchanting discoveries and unknown harmonies; so that loss and gain are cancelled off, and I need not discuss them further.) But all the innumerable beauties which will remain forever in the mind, all the potential graces which metre, the duty of rhyming, and the incomprehensible rule of hiatus definitely prevent from being realized, seem to constitute an immense loss, over which one can truly lament. Let us try instead to rejoice: the philosopher should always attempt to change a loss into the appearance of a loss. If only we reflect, if we go more deeply into a subject, we often succeed in making our first ideas of loss and gain, in ideal matters, seem absurd.

A hundred figures of clay, however perfectly moulded, do not present the same clear idea as a single figure of marble almost as beautiful. The first are more fragile than ourselves; the second is a little more enduring. We imagine how it resisted the sculptor; it did not wish to emerge from its crystallized shadows. Long days were the price of this mouth and of these arms. An artist struck thousands of rebounding blows, each a slow question of the future form. The dense and pure shadow fell in splinters, fled in glittering dust. A man advanced against a stone; time was his tool;

he crept painfully along the side of a mistress profoundly slumbering in the future; he traced the contours of this creature he had slowly made his own; at last she detached herself from the mass of the universe and the vagueness of an idea. Here at last she stands, a monster of grace and hardness, born, for an indeterminate time, from the energy and perseverance of a single thought. These so rebellious unions are the most precious of all. Take this weakness for sign of a great soul: that it wishes to draw from itself some object which will astonish, resemble, and confound itself; something more pure, more incorruptible, and to some degree more necessary than the very being which was its author.

But the great soul produces of itself only the mixture of its facility and richness, between which two it can hardly distinguish; it mirrors back its own good and its own evil; it does what it wishes, but wishes only those actions of which it is capable; it is free, but not sovereign. You must try, O Psyche! to exhaust all your facility against an obstacle; confront the obduracy of granite, chafe against your difficulties, and for a time despair. See how your vain enthusiasms grow cold, and your intentions are baffled! Perhaps you are not yet disciplined, and still prefer your self-indulgence to your resoluteness. Do you find this stone too hard, or dream of something pliable as wax, and the obedience of clay? But follow the path of your exasperated thought, and soon you will meet with this infernal inscription: *There is nothing so lovely as that which does not exist.*

The laws of a strict prosody are the artifice which endows our natural speech with the qualities of a resistant matter, foreign to our souls and deaf, as it were, to our desires. If these laws were not partly unreasonable, and if they did not goad us to revolt, they would be totally absurd. We can no longer do everything, once they are accepted; we can no longer say everything, and to say anything whatsoever, it no longer suffices to conceive the idea strongly, to be full of it, intoxicated with it, to allow a figure already finished in our absence to escape from the mystical moment. To a god alone is reserved the ineffable confusion of thought and act. As for us, we must toil, we must learn painfully to know their difference. We must pursue words which do not always exist, and chimerical resemblances; we must maintain ourselves in the

midst of impotence, labouring to unite sounds and
meanings, and in daylight creating one of those
nightmares which exhaust the dreamer, when he
struggles endlessly to equalize two phantoms whose
lines are unstable as his own. And so we must
passionately wait, change hours and days as one
would change a tool—and wish, wish . . . and
even, not wish excessively.

Being free today of all obligatory force and all
false necessity, these old inflexible laws have no
other virtue than to define, and define very simply,
an absolute world of expression. This at least is
the new meaning I find in them. We have resolved to subject nature—I mean the language—to
other rules than its own; they are unnecessary, but
they are ours; and we even carry our resolution to
the point of no longer deigning to invent them;
we accept them such as they are.

They form a sharp division between that which
exists of itself and that which specially exists because of ourselves alone. Here is something
strictly human: a decree. But our delights do not
perish, nor our emotions languish, when subjected
to this decree; they are both multiplied and created

by conventional disciplines. Gamblers might serve for example. Consider the pain they are caused and the ardour with which they are fired by their curious systems and the fantastic restrictions they place on their acts. They are absolutely convinced that the little ivory ball is influenced by their placing a bet in a certain square; they feel magnetic fields and invisible forces which the laws of physics do not recognize. This magnetism disappears with the game. The excessive concentration which had kept it in existence for so long a time changes its nature, dissolving like a dream. . . . The reality of dreams exists in man alone.

Understand me clearly. I do not say that "pathless delight" is not the principle and the very aim of the poet's art. I do not disparage the resplendent gift which our life makes to our consciousness when, with one sudden gesture, it pours forth a thousand memories. However, since the beginnings of literature, there has been no chance discovery or collection of such discoveries which has seemed to constitute a work of art.

I only wished to show that all this tyranny—obligatory metres, rhymes, fixed forms—when adopted once for all and opposed to ourselves, possesses a philosophic beauty of its own. These chains which tighten at every movement of our genius remind us, instantly, of all the contempt which is the just portion of that familiar chaos called, by the vulgar, *thought*—without their being aware that its *natural* conditions are no less accidental, no less futile, than those of a charade.

Conscious poetry is the art of a profound sceptic. It presupposes an extraordinary freedom with regard to the totality of our ideas and sensations. The gods, graciously, give us a first verse *for nothing;* but it is our task to fashion the second, which must harmonize with the first and not be too unworthy of its supernatural brother. All the resources of thought and experience are required to render it comparable to the verse which was a gift.

Only a singularly observant mind, rich in delicacies and researches, could be the author of *Adonis*. The La Fontaine who was able, a little later, to write such admirably varied verses, was able to write them only at the end of twenty years devoted to symmetrical measures; *Adonis* is the best of these exercises. Meanwhile he was giving the observers of his own time a spectacle of naïvety and idleness which, turned naïvely and idly into a tradition, has come down to our own days.

Literary history, like other histories, is woven of diversely gilded legends. The most fallacious are necessarily due to the most faithful witnesses. Who could be more misleading than those truthful men who confine themselves to telling what they saw, as if we had seen it ourselves? But precisely how are we affected by what we see? One of the most serious and logical men I ever knew generally appeared to be the soul of levity; a second nature clothed him with nonsense. And our minds are like our bodies in this respect: whatever they feel to be most important, they wrap in mystery and hide from themselves; they distinguish and defend it by placing it at a depth. Everything which matters is well hidden; witnesses and documents obscure it; acts and works are expressly designed to disguise it.

Did Racine himself know where he found the inimitable voice, the delicate pattern of inflection, the transparent mode of discourse, all the qualities which make him Racine, and without which he would be reduced to that inconsiderable personage of whom biographers relate a great number of facts—hardly more true of him than of ten thousand other Frenchmen? It is seldom that the lessons which literary history claims to teach have any bearing on the secret of how poems are made. Everything takes place within the artist, as if the observable events of his life had only a superficial influence on his works. The one important fact— the very act of the Muses—is independent of adventures, of the author's mode of life, of incidents, and of anything that could figure in a biography. Everything which history can observe is unimportant.

The essentials of his work are indefinable circumstances, occult encounters, facts visible to one man only, and others which are so easy or familiar to this one man that he disregards them. By examining ourselves, we can easily discover that these incessant and impalpable events are the solid matter of our true personality.

Every creative being is half certain, half uncertain, of his own powers; he feels a known and an unknown, whose incessant relations and unex-

pected exchanges finally give birth to some production. I do not know what I shall do; yet my
mind thinks that it knows itself, and I build and
count on this knowledge, which I call *myself*.
But *I shall surprise myself;* if I doubted this, I
should be nothing. I know that I shall be astonished by this or that thought which will soon occur
to me—and yet I demand this surprise; I build and
count on it, as I count on my certainty. I hope
for something unexpected which I shall create; I
have need of my known and my unknown.

How, then, can we conceive of the true creator
of a great work? But he simply does not exist.
How can the Self be defined if it changes sides
and opinions so often in the course of my work
that the work is disfigured under my hands; if
every repentance results in immense modifications;
and if a thousand accidents of memory, attention,
or sensation, occurring to my mind, appear at last
in my finished work as the essential ideas and original objects of my efforts? And yet all these accidents are surely of myself, since my strength and
weakness, my repetitions, my mannerisms, my
lights and shadows, can always be recognized in
whatever falls from my hands.

Let us despair of having clear vision in these matters, and soothe ourselves with an image. I can imagine this poet, his mind full of ruses and resources, pretending to sleep in the imaginary centre of his still uncreated work, better to capture that moment of his own greatest power which is his prey. In the vague depth of his eyes, all the forces of his desire and all the springs of his instinct are stretched taut. And there, intent on the chances from which she selects her nourishment; there, very obscure in the midst of the nets which she has woven out of words, and the secret lyres whose interwoven strings hum vaguely, a mysterious Arachne, muse of the hunt, watches in silence.

Predestined to be united by the soft and voluptuous euphony of their Greek [1] and Latin names, Venus and Adonis meet by the banks of a brook, where one of them is dreaming:

Il ne voit presque pas l'onde qu'il considère; [2]

and the other halts, descending from her chariot.

Venus is pretty well known. No quality of

---

[1] But the Greek name of Adonis is derived from a Semitic name.
[2] "Hardly he sees the wave before his eyes."

charm is lacking from this purely sensual abstraction, unless it be the very quality she came flying here to seek.

It is extremely difficult to paint a Venus. She is the sum of all perfections, and hence it is almost impossible to render her truly seductive. We are never attracted by this supreme degree of beauty or by such abstract graces; what charms us in a person is always a particular trait.

As for the Adonis toward whom she hastens, and by whom she desires to be loved, he has none of the qualities, in La Fontaine, of the adolescent mystic once worshipped in Byblos. He is only a very handsome young man of whom one can say very little, once he has been admired. Doubtless one can expect him to perform only such magnificent and agreeable acts as will suffice the Muses and satisfy the Goddess. He is here to love and then to die: there is no need of intelligence for these two great things.

We should not be surprised by the great simplicity of the hero and heroine; always the principal characters of a poem are the sweetness and vigour of the verse.

The happiness of our lovers is beyond compare. There is no attempt to describe it; the author must avoid being insipid and guard himself from crudity. What can the poet do, except to trust in poetry alone and make use of a delicately orchestrated music to hint at all the things we know, at all the things of which we need merely be reminded?

To Venus, although so lovely and apparently so content, there occurs the reflection that a particle, a mere pinch, of philosophy would spoil her happiness not in the least. A delight which is shared, or rather doubled, by two lovers, always runs the risk of a slight monotony. Two people who mutually arouse almost the same delights will sometimes end by finding each other too entirely similar. A man and woman at the summit of their happiness compose a sort of echo—or, what amounts to the same thing—a group of parallel mirrors; Baudelaire called them twins.[3]

In this respect the goddess gives evidence of a subtlety which she may have acquired in the course of her quarrels with Minerva. She has realized that love cannot be endless, if it confines itself to the

[3] *Dans nos deux esprits, ces miroirs jumeaux.*—"*La Mort des Amants.*"

act of ending as often as it can. One sees only too well that the minds of most lovers are as naturally foreign as their bodies are familiar. They know each other's likes and dislikes, which have been paired or harmoniously united; but they know nothing, and even wish to know nothing, of each other's metaphysics and special interests, except in so far as the latter can be promptly utilized. But love without the mind, if it is reciprocated and if nothing interferes with its course, is hardly more than a regular occupation. Either misfortunes or ideas are necessary.

Venus, in any case, risks a few reflections on change and permanence. Evidently she has read very little on this grave subject. Neither Heracleitus nor Zeno had been born. Kant, along with Aristotle and the abstruse M. Minkovski, lay jumbled in the anachronism of the future. Nevertheless she remarked with great exactness that time never flows back to its source; but how grievous was her error when she spoke this lovely verse:

Vainement pour les dieux il fuit d'un pas léger! [4]

She could hardly have foreseen the destruction

---

[4] "Vainly for the gods Time flees with airy tread."

of her finest temples and the decay of her cult; I mean, of her public cult.

Adonis does not listen. They return to pleasure for its own sake, and of this even the poet is a little weary:

> *Il est temps de passer au funeste moment*
> *Où la triste Vénus doit quitter son amant.* [5]

This rapid platitude is a very apparent sign of weariness. It is true that, in verse, everything which is necessary to say is almost impossible to say well.

And so Venus must depart; she must go to Paphos to disprove the current rumour that the goddess has ceased to protect her worshippers. It is strange that she should set so much store on being worshipped, at a moment when she loves and is loved in return.

But vanity, and those silly trifles we take for the obligations of our rank, will always persuade us to desert our den or chamber—in this case represented by a lovely wood. No one has yet been found,

[5] "Now to the fatal moment we pass over
When mournful Venus must forsake her lover."

even among the gods, who was brave enough to make sport of his disciples. And as for disdaining his own altars and sanctuaries, the burnt offerings which are there consumed, and the sermons and incense which rise from them—as for detesting flattery and reaching such a point of disgust that he rains fire and misfortune on all those heads which only by fear and their desperate hopes have been turned toward things divine, I never heard of a deity who took this firm resolve. Their fondness for us mortals is beyond my understanding.

It is so with Venus. Although she is wildly happy and almost omnipotent, she will leave Adonis for a time, in order not to offend her clientele of zealots. If there were no such caprices, there would be no gods, perhaps no poems, and assuredly no women.

She gives a thousand directions to the lover whose duties are so futilely suspended. The little speech in which she warns him against the two imaginable dangers—that he perish and that he be unfaithful—is beautifully proportioned. I have specially remarked one lovely verse, where all the great art and abstract power of Corneille come suddenly to light. After entreating Adonis not to become attached to the wood-nymphs, she says:

Leurs fers après les miens ont pour vous de la honte.[6]

What a splendid farewell was theirs! Only eight lines, but they are marvellous; or rather the passage is a marvel of eight lines, something almost infinitely rarer and more astonishing than eight fine lines. Only La Fontaine could have separated two beings so tenderly, and, by this pure act of rending apart, have added anything whatever to our image of their former joy. Making use of a refinement not often to be encountered in French poetry, La Fontaine here echoes, as if in the corresponding minor, the motif of the delicious moments he had described a short time before. These he had granted to his hero:

Jours devenus moments, moments filés de soie . . .[7]

And now he withdraws his gift:

Moments pour qui le sort rend vos vœux superflus,
Délicieux moments, vous ne reviendrez plus! [8]

2

[6] "Having served *me*, their favours are your shame."
[7] "Days that were moments, moments spun of silk."
[8] "Moments when fortune lavished all its store,
    Delicious moments, you will return no more!"

Adonis now suffers all the pangs of absence.

That is, he counts over, one by one, all the perfections of the happiness he lost but a moment since. When bodies are kept apart, our thoughts are busy with the contrast between the two realities which dispute the soul; we remember even those delights which we had scarcely perceived; the past which returns seems richer than the forgotten present from which it derives; time and distance serve to tighten, with growing cruelty, the bonds once imperceptibly woven by each caress. Adonis is like a falling stone arrested in its motion; during the fall it had ceased to weigh. If a stone could feel, it would suffer on the instant all the violent effects of suddenly halted movement; and in addition to this, would be conscious of all its weight, which it had practically lost, having been free to obey the law of gravity. In the same way the feeling of love, which is weakened by possession, is developed by loss and privation. To possess is to think no more of love, but to lose is to possess indefinitely in the mind.

Adonis, being unhappy, was on the point of becoming intelligent. A season too warm and voluptuous often leaves terrible memories behind; these were deepening and developing his mind; they had led him to the threshold of the most fundamental doubts; and he was menaced with those inner difficulties which, because they divide our emotions, force us to invent our intelligence.

Adonis was going to have ideas, and hastened to call his huntsmen. Better to die than to reflect.

It must be confessed that this ill-omened hunt is the weak part of the poem. It is almost as fatal to the author as it will be to the hero.

How go about describing a hunt? The authors of the sixteenth and seventeenth centuries who have treated this fine subject have left passages admirable for their vigour and precision (and hence for their style). From one of these writers, not the most famous, Victor Hugo did not disdain to borrow a whole page of magnificent French, which he inserted textually, or nearly so, in his charming tale of Pécopin the Fair and the Fair Bauldour. But La Fontaine, in spite of his official post as Master of Streams and Forests, has nothing to offer here but a purely rhetorical venery. In default of a hunt described according to the ancient rules of sport, one might have expected I do not know what sylvan fantasy from this future animator of furred and feathered creatures. One can easily imagine how the man designed by the gods to write the *Fables* could have treated all these beasts in movement—some of them urged on and lashed, others tracked down and hunted out, all beside themselves, the dogs baying, the huntsmen galloping and sounding their horns. He might have invented the thoughts and conversations of these actors; while the remarks of the feathered creatures, safe spectators in their trees, would have been a natural artifice to inform us of the day's events. All these elementary souls, their arguments and stratagems, the passions which fill their souls, the rôle men play in this rude pleasure—the *Fables* are full of themes like these; and by combining them, La Fontaine might have written an infinitely new and diverting chase.

But he does not seem to have realized that he was almost touching, here, the territory which should be his a little later. Far from feeling that his subject was guiding him to the borders of his natural kingdom, he was obviously bored when he elaborated the three hundred verses which the hunt obliged him to write. Now, a yawn is not so far from a laugh that the two are never curiously mingled. They have a common frontier, and as this is approached the absurdity of acting against one's wishes is easily turned into burlesque action. And so, if I find essentially comic verses in a development which admits of nothing humorous, and even on the occasion of grave and fatal accidents, I conclude that the weary author is suddenly taking revenge on himself for his too eagerly accepted task and his voluntary pains. A bit of humour escapes inevitably. Laughter and yawns surprise us in a *flagrante delicto* of refusal.

Before the huntsmen pass in their train, we shall be diverted by certain caricatures. One of them pleases me more than a little, although all its humour lies in the sonority of the verse:

> *On y voit arriver Bronte au cœur indomptable.*[9]

It was also necessary to describe the monster— a very terrible boar, one of those beasts which hunt alone and rely only on their tusks; its fierce blows

[9] "And now comes Bronte of the undauntable heart."

will disembowel the horses and wound the mastiffs "in the trunk of their body."

However terrifying a monster may be, the task of describing it is a little more terrifying than the beast itself. It is a known fact that such unhappy monsters have never been able to play more than a ridiculous rôle in the arts. I can think of no monster painted, sung, or carved which has succeeded in making us preserve our gravity, to say nothing of arousing the slightest fear. The great fish which devoured the prophet Jonah, and a little later, in the same waters, swallowed the adventurous Sinbad; this same beast which, at another stage of its career, was perhaps the saviour and ferry of Arion; in spite of its great courtesy and that scrupulous sense of honour which made it deposit its dinners of distinguished men so exactly on the beach, returning them in such excellent condition to their studies and occupations at the very destination they had proposed to reach; although this monster was not intended to be feared, but rather was officious and good-hearted, none the less it seems infinitely ridiculous. And see this extravagantly composite animal which the gold-armoured Roger of Ingres' painting is transfixing at the feet of lovely Angelica; imagine the porpoise or sea-cow whose sudden snorts and brutal games in the foam of the breakers have just frightened the steeds of Hippolytus; hear Fafnir, the lamentable cuckold, braying in the depths of his cave—never have these been able to win a little terror from their audience, even by way of charity. They can only console themselves by this observation: that more human monsters, Quasimodo, Gwinplaine, the Cyclops, and their sort, have found little more credit and authority than themselves. The necessary complement of a monster is a child's brain.

This curse of being absurd, which is greater for them than the curse of being monsters, seems to arise not so much from the impotence of their inventors as from their own nature and extraordinary vocation, as you will easily be convinced by even a short visit to the museum. There you will see authentic monsters, combining wings and weight, a very slender neck with a ponderous belly; there you will find real dragons, sea serpents which existed, hydras traced on slate, gigantic turtles with the head of a pig, all the successive populations which have inhabited the uneasy storeys of our dwelling, but have ceased to please this planet—and all suggesting, to our here and now, the grotesque element of nature. They are like anatomical engravings. We did not believe that our world was so bizarre; and our final solution is a feeling of the improbable and a reflection on the awkwardness and primitive stupidity which can be measured only by a laugh.

Enough of this monster. And let us pass over the rather spiritless struggle which follows. One couplet, however, I should like to quote; it is charming in execution, and its ironical music has always amused me:

> *Nisus, ayant cherché son salut sur un arbre,*
> *Rit de voir ce chasseur plus froid que n'est un marbre.*[10]

The water nymphs, vaguely resembling in their conduct, as they do in their fluid morals and uncertain nature, those madcap maidens of the Rhine who once endeavoured, under other skies, to save the hardy Siegfried—the nymphs attempt to preserve Adonis, but in vain. They know that heroes always run headlong toward disaster, but still they try to make this hero lose his path and fail his

[10] "Safe in the refuge of the branches, Nisus
Laughed to see this huntsman cold as ice is."

88

rendezvous with death. They oppose the Fates
with the loveliest verses in the world:

Les nymphes, de qui l'œil voit les choses futures,
L'avaient fait égarer en des routes obscures.
Le son des cors se perd par un charme inconnu . . .[11]

The Fates are deaf to verse; otherwise their very
name would long since have fallen from the dictionary of current words. Nor have the Naiads
any power over the soul of this traveller who fares
toward death. Adonis must perish; all paths will
lead him to this goal. He enters the heat of the
chase, impatient to avenge his friend Palmyrus,
who has just been slightly injured; he makes a
charge, wounds, is wounded. The monster and
the hero expire, but they expire in the grand manner. Here is the dying boar:

Ses yeux d'un somme dur sont pressés et couverts,
Il demeure plongé dans la nuit la plus noire.[12]

And as for Adonis:

On ne voit plus l'éclat dont sa bouche était peinte,
On ne voit que les traits . . .[13]

[11] "The nymphs, who hold the future in their gaze,
  Led him to wander in uncertain ways.
  The horns are muffled by an unknown spell. . . ."
[12] "A pitiless sleep weighs down and hides his eyes,
  Wrapped in the nethermost depths of night he lies."
[13] "The splendour has departed from his face,
  Only the lineaments are seen. . . ."

Venus instructed by the winds, Venus having hastened broken-hearted to the spot, can only sing her despair, a task which she fulfils divinely. Nothing could be more lovely than the opening and development of this final movement; and, from another point of view, I find a curious importance in her polished lament. This passage of perhaps forty verses is distinguished by all the qualities which will finally be Racine's, but only after many years. If the creator of Phædra had thought of bringing her to the corpse of Hippolytus, and of making her breathe out her grief, I am not certain that he could have rendered its tones more pure, or have made the despairing queen deliver a more harmonious lament.

It must be noted that *Adonis* was written about 1657, perhaps twelve years before the genius of Racine reached its maturity; also that the tone, the transitions, the monumental profile, and even the sonority of the funeral oration we have been discussing, are sometimes indistinguishable from those we admire in Racine's best tragedies.

Who is the author of verses like these?

Mon amour n'a donc pu vous faire aimer la vie!
Tu me quittes, cruel! Au moins ouvre les yeux,

Montre-toi plus sensible à mes tristes adieux;
Vois de quelle douleur ton amante est atteinte!
Hélas! J'ai beau crier: il est sourd à ma plainte.
Une éternelle nuit l'oblige à me quitter. . . .[14]

Encor si je pouvais le suivre en ces lieux sombres!
Que ne m'est-il permis d'errer parmi les ombres. . . .

Je ne demandais pas que la Parque cruelle
Prît à filer leur trame une peine éternelle;
Bien loin que mon pouvoir l'empêchât de finir,
Je demande un moment et ne puis l'obtenir. . . .

And the rest. One might easily mistake the
name of the author.

Acante (such was the name La Fontaine gave to
Racine)—Acante was nineteen at the time when
these verses could first have been read. Many
people must have known of them, if not from the
celebrated manuscript which is the masterpiece of

[14] "My loving could not grant you love of life;
Heartless you quit me. If at least your eyes
Opened in answer to my sad goodbyes,
Saw how their mistress suffered! But in vain
I weep; he does not heed my pain.
Eternal night has snatched him from my side. . . ."
[15] "If only I could seek those sombre glades,
With him to wander in the realm of shades. . . ."
[16] "The harshest of the Fates from out her skein
To choose an eternal thread of love and pain,
I did not ask, nor power to make him live;
I begged a moment, and she did not give. . . ."

Nicolas Jarry, the calligrapher, then at least from the copies which would pass from hand to hand and circulate from group to group, from salon to salon.

I should not like to wager that Racine could not recite our *Adonis* by heart.

Perhaps those accents of Venus may have given the initial tone to that pure voice whose praises I was singing a little while since. Perhaps this is how it first became conscious of its own power. Little more is required to engender a great man from a young man ignorant of his gifts. The greatest, and even the holiest, had need of precursors.

It is natural and absurd to regret the splendid dreams which were never realized. We still believe that they were possible, long after the event has shown that they had no place in the world. This curious feeling is almost inseparable from our attitude to history; we regard the course of time as a highway, at every point of which there is a cross-roads. . . .

For my part, when reading *Adonis*, I regret all the hours wasted by La Fontaine on that quantity of *Tales* which he produced. I cannot bear their false and rustic tone, their general vulgarity, and all the boredom which clings to a smuttiness so contrary to passion and so mortal to poetry. Verses like these are repugnantly facile:

> *Nos deux époux, à ce que dit l'histoire,*
> *Sans disputer n'étaient pas un moment....*[17]

Still more I regret the poems like *Adonis* which he might have bequeathed us, instead of those wearisome *Tales*. What idylls and eclogues was he not born to write! Chénier, who attempted the task with such success, and who derives in some measure from La Fontaine, does not entirely console us for this imaginary loss. His genius seems more slender, less pure, and less mysterious than that of our author. We can see its methods more clearly.

La Fontaine's *Adonis* was written about two hundred and sixty years ago. During this time, the French language has not remained the same. Besides, the reader of today is very far from the

[17] "For man and wife, if all the tales be true,
A moment never passed without a quarrel...."

reader of 1660; he has other memories and quite another "sensibility." His culture, too, is different, granting that he has a culture; sometimes he has several, and it happens occasionally that he has none at all. He has lost and gained; he no longer belongs to the same species. However, the most important ingredient of literary composition is the idea of the *most probable reader;* and it is from the conception which he has necessarily formed of this reader that the author's mind, consciously or unconsciously, eagerly or against his will, may be said to *take its pitch.* Hence, the change of century, which means a change of reader, is comparable to an alteration in the text itself, always incalculable and always unforeseen.

Let us rejoice that we can still read *Adonis,* and read nearly all of it with delight; but do not think we are reading the same poem that was known to contemporaries of the author. Perhaps the qualities they prized most highly are those which escape us; others which they hardly perceived may affect us deeply. A few charming things have become profound, while some have grown insipid. Consider the mixture of enthusiasm and dislike which this text can arouse in a modern reader, nourished

on the poetry of our age; all these readings in contemporary authors have harmonized his mind with
theirs; like his ear it has become sensitive to impressions which the author of another century
never thought to produce, and insensible to effects
which he studied with care.   Racine, for example,
when he wrote his illustrious line—

   Dans l'Orient désert, quel devint mon ennui! [18]

—never imagined that he was expressing anything
else than a lover's despair.   But the magnificent
harmony of these three words, when time had prolonged it through the nineteenth century, gained
unexpected strength and an extraordinary resonance from romantic poetry; in the sensibility of
our time it is wonderfully mingled with some of
Baudelaire's finest lines.   Detached from Anti-
ochus, the friend of Titus and lover of Berenice,
it becomes a pure and nostalgic generality; its
finished elegance is transformed into infinite
beauty.   And, if this "deserted," this "Orient,"
this "ennui," combined under Louis XIV., have

[18] Literally and baldly: "In the deserted Orient, how great was my
ennui!"   *Ennui,* in the seventeenth century, was used in its original
sense of "keen torment."   *Tr.*

acquired a limitless meaning and the power of a magic spell, it is through the existence of another century, which can conceive of them only in its own colour.

The same applies to *Adonis*. What pleasure can we take in this gallant tale today? It is revivified, perhaps, by the contrast of its own sweet form and clearer melodies with our modern system of discordance, and this tradition of excess which we accept with such docility. Our dazzled eyes demand a rest from melting graces and transparent shadows; our scorched palates will find, perhaps, some strangeness in pure water. We might even happen to discover that good writing has a fascination of its own.

A FOREWORD

This Foreword appeared in a volume of poems by M. Lucien Fabre, *La Connaissance de la Déesse*, published in 1920.

A FOREWORD

DURING the last forty years a doubt has disappeared from the mind. The ancient ambition of squaring the circle has been shown, by conclusive demonstration, to be an impossible dream. Happy are the geometricians, who from time to time resolve some nebula of their system, but poets are less happy; they are not yet convinced of the impossibility of *squaring* all thoughts into poetic form.

Since the process by which our desire succeeds in constructing an harmonious and unforgettable figure of speech is very secret and very complex, we are still permitted, and will always be permitted, to doubt whether theory, science, history, politics, morality, apologetics, and, in general, all the subjects of prose cannot assume the musical and personal garb of a poem. It would only be a question of talent; there is no absolute rule against it. Description and generalization, the anecdote with its pointed moral, information, controversy— all intellectual matters have, at some time in the course of the ages, been chained to rhythm and subjected by art to curious—to divine—conditions.

Neither the proper end of poetry nor the methods to attain this end being elucidated—the initiate being silent and the ignorant expounding their theories at length—all distinct ideas on these questions remain personal, the greatest contrariety of opinions is permitted, and each opinion is supported by illustrious examples and experiments difficult to contest.

Favoured by this uncertainty, the production of poems on every variety of subject has continued till our day; one can even say that the greatest, and perhaps the most admirable, of the versified works which have come down to us belong to the didactic or historical order. *De Rerum Natura,* the *Georgics,* the *Æneid,* the *Divine Comedy, La Légende des Siècles* . . . derive part of their substance and their interest from notions which could be expressed in the most indifferent prose. They can be translated without being rendered entirely insignificant.

It was only to be expected that a time would come when the vast systems of this nature would give way before specialization. Since one could read them in several different ways, each independent of the others, or separate them into distinct moments of our attention, this plurality of readings would some day lead to what was, in effect, a division of work. It was in this manner that the consideration of a given body gave rise in the course of time to the diversity of the sciences.

Finally, toward the middle of the nineteenth century, French literature saw the birth of a remarkable ambition—that of definitely isolating poetry from every essence other than its own. This almost chemical preparation of poetry in its pure state had been predicted and recommended with the greatest precision by Edgar Allan Poe. And so it is not surprising to see, in Baudelaire, the commencement of this struggle for a self-contained perfection.

To Baudelaire also belongs another innovation. He was the first of our poets to undergo the influence of music; to invoke it and to ask it questions. Through Berlioz and Wagner, romantic music had sought the effects of literature, and had obtained them to a greater degree. Its success is not difficult to explain, when one considers that the violence, if not the frenzy, which was in the taste of the time, and the romantic exaggeration of depth, distress, brilliance, or purity could hardly be translated into speech without falling into the ridiculous, and without being involved in many absurdities insoluble in terms of time; these elements of ruin are less perceptible in music than in poetry. Perhaps this is because music carries with it a sort of life, which it imposes on us by physical law; whereas the monuments of literature demand that we endow them with this life.

Whatever the case may be, a time arrived when poetry felt itself grow weak and pale before the energies and resources of the orchestra. Even on hearing the richest or most resounding poem by Victor Hugo, we are far from feeling those extreme illusions, those shivers, those transports, and, in the quasi-intellectual order, those false lucidities, those special types of thought, those images of a fabulous mathematics made real, which the symphony liberates, suggests, or thunders forth; which it weakens to the point of silence, or annihilates with a single chord, leaving us with the extraordinary impression of omnipotence and falsehood. . . . Never, perhaps, have the promises of eternity which poets have received since the childhood of the world and of language, or their immemorial possession of the lyre, or the confidence they place in their particular genius, or this first rank which they claim to occupy in the hierarchy of the servants of the universe—never have these riches, the heritage of poets, seemed so definitely menaced. They would leave the concert overwhelmed. Overwhelmed—dazzled; as if, having been carried to the seventh heaven by a cruel boon, they had reached these summits only to be granted the luminous contemplation of forbidden possibilities, of inimitable marvels. And, as these imperious delights grew keener and more incontestable, the torture of their pride became more immediate, its sufferings more hopeless.

Pride gave them counsel. Pride, for intellectual men, is a vital necessity.

To each according to his nature, it breathed the spirit of struggle—a strange intellectual struggle. All methods known to the art of verse, all the artifices of rhetoric and prosody were recalled, and many an invention was summoned to appear before the exacerbated consciousness.

The movement christened *Symbolism* can be

very simply explained by the ambition—common to several families of poets, which incidentally were mutually hostile—"to reconquer, from Music, that which was theirs." The secret of this movement is nothing else. The oddities and obscurities for which it was so bitterly attacked; its apparently too intimate relations with English, Slavic, or Germanic literatures; its disorderly syntax, irregular rhythms, curious vocabulary, continual metaphors . . . all can be easily deduced as soon as the principle is recognized. It was useless for those who witnessed these experiments, and even those who performed them, to lay all the burden on this poor word, "symbol." The word contains only what you will; if some one endows it with his own aspirations, he can rediscover them there!—But we were nourished on music, and our literary minds could only dream of deriving almost the same effects from words that were being produced on our nervous systems by purely auditory agents. Some of us cherished Wagner and others Schumann. I might have written instead that we hated Wagner or Schumann. When interest rises to fever heat, these two emotions are indistinguishable.

To list and explain the tendencies of that period would require a systematic treatise. More fervour, courage, and learning; more researches into theory, more disputes, and a more pious attention have rarely been devoted, in so short a time, to the problem of pure beauty. One might say that the problem was attacked from all sides. Language is the most complex of mediums, and its multiple nature permitted experiments of different types. Some, who preserved the traditional forms of French verse, studied to eliminate descriptions, maxims, morals, and arbitrary precision; their poetry was purged of almost all those intellectual elements which music is unable to express. Others endowed all objects with infinite meanings which presupposed a hidden metaphysics. The machinery of their poems was ambiguous and charming. Their enchanted parks and evanescent forests were peopled with a purely imaginary fauna. Everything was allusion; nothing was content simply to *be*. In those mirror-haunted kingdoms, everything thought; or at least everything appeared to think. . . . Elsewhere a few magicians, more headstrong and argumentative, were attacking the old prosody. For some of these experimenters, auditory colour and the art of combining alliterations seemed to have no more secrets; they would deliberately transpose the timbres of the orchestra into their verse, and their attempts were not always mistaken. Others went studiously searching after the simplicity and artless graces of the old ballads. Philology and phonetics were summoned to the eternal debates of these stern lovers of the Muse.

It was a time of theories, curiosity, glosses, and passionate explanations. There was a certain austerity about the new generation of poets. They rejected scientific dogma, which was beginning to be unfashionable, and did not accept religious dogma, which had not yet become the mode. In the profound and scrupulous worship of all the arts, they thought to have found a discipline, and perhaps a truth, beyond the reach of doubt. A kind of religion was very nearly established. . . . But these aims are not explicit in the poems themselves. Instead of reading them to find a theory of art, we must carefully observe what they forbade—the notions which ceased to appear in poetry during the period under discussion. Thus, it would seem that abstract thought, formerly admitted into the realm of verse, had become almost impossible to combine with the immediate emotion which poets wished to arouse at every moment. Exiled from a poetry which wished to reduce itself to its own essence; frightened away by those multiplied effects of surprise and music which were demanded by the taste of the day, such thought took refuge in the phase of preparation and in the theory of the poem. Philosophy and even ethics tended to abandon the work of art and confine themselves to the reflections preceding the work.

In this respect there was a very real progress. Philosophy, when vague ideas and refuted ideas have been eliminated, is now reduced to five or six problems, apparently exact, but fundamentally indeterminate. They can be denied at will, can always be reduced to linguistic quarrels, and depend for their solution on our manner of *writing* them. But the interest of these curious labours is not diminished to the degree one might expect: it resides in this fragility and these very quarrels; that is, in the delicacy and increasing subtlety of the logical and psychological machinery which they force us to employ; the interest resides no longer in conclusions. Hence, to philosophize no longer means to express even the most admirable opinions

on nature and its Author, on life and death, on
time, on justice. . . . Our philosophy is defined
by its methods, and not by its object. It cannot be
separated from its own difficulties, which constitute its *form*; and it could not assume the *form* of
verse without losing its own character or corrupt-
ing that of verse. To speak of philosophical poetry
today—even when invoking Alfred de Vigny,
Leconte de Lisle, or a few others—means that one
is naïvely confusing modes and applications of
thought which are incompatible one with the other.
For is it not equivalent to forgetting that the aim of
one who speculates is to fix or to create a notion—in
other words a *power* and an *instrument of power*—
whereas the modern poet endeavours to produce
a *state* in the reader, and to carry this exceptional
state to the point of perfect delight? . . .

Such, in its general effects, when viewed from
the perspective of a quarter-century and separated
from our own day by an abyss of events, was the
great purpose of the Symbolists. I do not know
which of their multiform efforts the future will
preserve, nor is it always a lucid and equitable
judge. Endeavours like theirs can never be free

from audacities, risks, exaggerated cruelties, and a
bit of childishness. . . . Tradition, intelligibil-
ity, and spiritual balance, which are the usual victims of the mind struggling toward some object,
have suffered at times from our devotion to the
purest beauty. Sometimes we were vague, and
sometimes puerile. Our style was not always so
worthy of praise and permanence as our ambition
desired; and our innumerable theses, in melancholy
throng, people the mild infernos of our memory.
. . . As for our works and opinions, our technical
preferences, there let them rest! But our Idea
itself, and our Sovereign Good, are these no more
today than the pale elements of forgetfulness?
Must we to this point perish! How perish, O
comrades?—What doubt has so secretly under-
mined our certainties, diminished our truth, dispersed our courage? Has it been discovered that
light can grow old? And how is it possible—herein lies the mystery—that those who followed us,
and having been devalued and disillusioned by a
similar change, like us will pass—that these successors could have other desires than ours, and other
gods? It appeared to us so clearly that there was
no flaw in our ideal! Was it not derived from all

the experience of all former literatures? Was it not the supreme and miraculously delayed flower of all the profundity of culture?

Two explanations can be offered for this apparent ruin. First, one might decide that we were simply the victims of a mental illusion. When this had vanished, we were left only with the memory of ridiculous actions and an incomprehensible passion. . . . But a desire cannot be illusory. Nothing is more specifically real than a desire, considered as desire; like the God of St. Anselm, its idea and its reality are indistinguishable. Hence we must seek elsewhere, and find a more ingenious argument for our ruin. Instead of its being illusory, we must suppose that our way was indeed the only way; that our desire was guiding us to the very essence of our art; and that we had actually deciphered the meaning of all the efforts of our ancestors, taken whatever seemed most magical in their work, formed our own road from these fragments, and followed this precious path to infinity, continually refreshed with palms and wells of sweet water; on the horizon, always, was pure poetry. There lay our peril; precisely there our ruin; and, in the same spot, our goal.

For a truth of this order is a limit of the world, and such a limit cannot be permanently attained. Nothing so pure can coexist with the conditions of life. We can only *traverse* the idea of perfection, much in the same fashion that we can pass our hands safely through a flame; but flame itself is uninhabitable, and the abodes of pure serenity are of necessity empty and desolate. I mean to say that our tendency toward the utmost rigour of art—toward a beauty always more conscious of its genesis, always more independent of all *subjects,* and free from sentimental or vulgar interest as from the coarse effects of eloquence—that all our too-conscious zeal was leading to an almost inhuman state. This is a general truth: metaphysics, ethics, and even the sciences have discovered it for themselves.

Absolute poetry can proceed only by exceptional marvels. The works which consist entirely of absolute poetry are the rarest and most improbable jewels to be found among the imponderable treasures of a literature. However, like a perfect vacuum and absolute zero—ideals which cannot be attained, and cannot even be approached save at the price of an exhausting progression of efforts—the final purity of our art demands, from those who conceive of this ideal, such long and rigorous discipline that all their natural joy in being poets is absorbed in the task, leaving only a pride in never being content. Most of the young men gifted with the poetic instinct find this austerity beyond their power to bear. Our successors did not envy us our torments; they did not adopt our delicacies; the poetic devices which we had accepted as new difficulties, they sometimes mistook for liberties; and at times they destroyed what we only aimed to dissect. In this way they opened their eyes once more to the accidents of life, whereas we had closed our eyes in order that we might resemble its essence. . . .

All this was to be expected. Even the events which followed were not impossible to foresee. Would not the attempt be made, some day, to unite our own past with this past which followed ours? Some doctrines could be taken from one, some from the other, so long as they were mutually consistent. Here and there, in a few minds, I can see the progress of this natural undertaking. Life proceeds in no other fashion; and the same process which can be observed in the succession of living creatures, this mixture of continuity and atavism, is also reproduced in the course of the literary life.

This topic is one I was discussing with M. Fabre. He had come that day to tell me about his studies and his verse, for his wise and clear mind had been inspired by I do not know what spirit of imprudence and error to question one which is neither wise nor clear. We both endeavoured to explain our views on poetry, and although this sort of conversation is easily lost among infinities, we managed not to stray from our path. This was because our different attitudes, each moving and changing behind its own impassable walls, succeeded nevertheless in preserving a remarkable correspondence. Thanks to a common vocabulary, the most exact in the world, we were continually able not to misunderstand each other. Algebra and geometry were the means which permitted us, from time to time, to exchange precise signals. I feel sure that the future will be able to construct a language for the intellect, based on these two sciences.

Meanwhile I had discovered, in my visitor, one of those minds to which my own is drawn. I love those poets who venerate the goddess too lucidly to

worship her with unguided thoughts and the surrender of their reason. They are convinced that
she does not demand the *sacrifizio dell'intelletto*.
Neither Minerva and Pallas nor radiant Apollo ap-
prove of those abominable mutilations which some
of their crazed worshippers inflict on the organism
of their thought; the gods repulse with horror
these bearers of a freshly torn and bleeding logic,
which they wish to sacrifice on the divine altars.
The real divinities have no desire for incomplete
victims. It is true that they require sacrifices;
this demand is common to all supreme powers, for
they must live; but they wish their victims to be
whole and without blemish.

With this truth M. Lucien Fabre is familiar. It
was not in vain that he acquired a singularly complete and solid culture. The art of the engineer,
to which he devotes not the best, but perhaps the
greatest portion of his time, demands a long course
of study and leads its more distinguished disciples
into complex activities. They must take charge of
men, mould and combine materials, and find satis-
factory solutions for unexpected problems involv-
ing the contrary demands of economics and civil
and natural laws. This sort of reasoning on com-

plex systems hardly lends itself to the assumption
of a general form.   There are no formulæ which
cover these individual cases, no equations possible
between these heterogeneous groups of data; little
can be done with certainty, and even to feel one's
way ahead is only lost time unless one is guided
by a very subtle sense of direction.   In the eyes
of an observer able to disregard appearances, this
activity, this tense waiting, these reflected hesita-
tions and sudden discoveries might justly be compared to the inner moments of a poet.   But I
am afraid that very few engineers suspect themselves of being as near as I suggest to the inventors
of figures and adjusters of words. . . . There are
not many more who have made profound researches into the metaphysics of the being, as M.
Fabre has done.   He is no stranger to philosophies.
Not even theology is beyond his interest.   He did
not believe that the intellectual world was so young
and limited as is popularly supposed; or perhaps it
was simply that his practical mind estimated the
smallness of a probability.   How can we believe,
without being strangely credulous, that the keenest brains of a dozen centuries wore themselves
fruitlessly away in vain and austere speculations?

Sometimes I think (but with shame, and in the depths of my heart) that a more or less distant future will regard the immense labours which have been performed, during our own time, on the *continuous*, the *transfinite*, and a few other mathematical concepts, with the same air of pity that we assume at the mention of scholasticism. . . . But the material of theology is certain texts, and M. Fabre did not even recoil before Hebrew!

This combination of qualities—a general culture along with habits of rigorous discipline, and a decisive sense of practical things along with a magnificently useless learning—bears witness to the existence of an organizing will which subjects them all to order. It happens that the order in question is that of poetry. The case is very remarkable, and one must expect that a mind so trained to such habits of distinctness will resume, according to its nature, the study of the eternal problems on which I said a few words, a few pages above. If such a mind were reduced to a purely technical intelligence, it would doubtless make brutal innovations and carry its rage for naïve inventions into an ancient art. Examples of the sort can be found; paper is all-suffering, and the

desire to astonish is the most natural, and the easiest to conceive, of all desires; it permits any reader,
even the humblest, to decipher without effort the
very simple secret of many surprising works. But
having reached a little higher degree of consciousness and knowledge, the poet comes to see that the
language is not so easily perfected; that prosody
has not lacked for suppliants or modes of supplica-
tion during the course of the ages; and he realizes
that all the attention and labour he can expend in
contradicting the results of so much accumulated
experience must necessarily be subtracted from his
other aims. The pleasure of not utilizing the
known can be gained only at an unknown price.
An architect can disdain the laws of statics, or attempt to revolt from the formulæ covering the
resistance of materials, but he is only defying probability; the penalty, a thousand chances to one,
will not be long to wait. The penalty in literature
is less appalling; it is also much less swift; but time,
in any case, will be quick enough to assume the
task of justice; it will answer our neglect of the
simplest rules of applied psychology by its own
neglect of our work. Hence, it is to our interest

to calculate our prudence and audacities with all possible precision.

M. Fabre, who is a good calculator, has not ignored the poet Lucien Fabre. When this latter decided to write a work of the most difficult and enviable type to be found in our art—that is, a system of poems forming a spiritual drama; a finished drama, the characters of which are the very forces of our soul—the standards and precisions of the engineer found a natural function in this construction. The reader will judge the success of this curiously audacious effort to endow philosophical essences, directly represented as such, with life and the most impassioned movement. Eros—an Eros very violent and lovely, but secretly enslaved by some Reason which unchains, as it can again imprison, his furies—is the true coryphæus of these poems. I will not say that this reason is never too clearly revealed in the diction. I felt it my duty to contest some of the words which M. Fabre has employed, for my part believing that they were too alien to the poetic language. This was a rather unstable reproach, for the poetic language changes like any other; and the geometrical terms which sometimes provoked my re-

sistance will perhaps melt at length, as so many
other technical words have done, into the abstract
and homogeneous metal of the language of the
gods.

However, before attempting to pass judgment
on a work, one must first of all consider the difficulties which the author has set for himself. A
statement of these voluntary restrictions, if one
succeeded in making such a list, would immediately
reveal the intellectual degree of the poet, the
quality of his pride, the delicacy and the despotism
of his nature. M. Fabre chose noble and rigorous
conditions; he desired that his emotions, intense as
they may appear in his verse, should be closely
co-ordinated among themselves, and subject to the
invisible empire of reason. Perhaps, in some places,
this shadowy, all-seeing queen is faced with dangers
and loses some share of her sovereignty—for, as
the author magnificently writes:

> The ardent flesh gnaws ceaselessly
> The bitter oaths which it has sworn.[1]

But what poet could complain of this?

[1] *L'ardente chair ronge sans cesse*
Les durs serments qu'elle a jurés.

119

ON POE'S "EUREKA"

To Lucien Fabre

I was twenty and believed in majesty of thought. I found it a strange torture to be, and not to be. At times I could feel infinite forces within me. They disappeared when faced with problems, and the weakness of my effective powers filled me with despair. I was moody, quick, tolerant in appearance, fundamentally hard, extreme in contempt, absolute in admiration, easy to impress, impossible to convince. I put my faith in a few ideas which had come to me. I regarded their conformity with the being which gave them birth as a certain indication of their universal value. Since they appeared so distinctly to my mind, they also appeared invincible; convictions born of desire are always the strongest.

I guarded these shadowy ideas as my secrets of state. I was ashamed of their strangeness; I feared they were absurd; I even knew they were absurd, but not entirely so. They were vain in themselves, but powerful by virtue of the remarkable force with which my confidence endowed me.

My jealous watch over this mystery of weakness filled me with a sort of vigour.

I had ceased to write verse, and had almost ceased to read. Novels and poems, in my opinion, were only impure and half-unconscious applications of a few properties inherent in the great secrets I hoped some day to reveal—basing this hope on the unremitting assurance that they must necessarily exist. As for philosophers, I had read them very little, and was irritated by that little, because they never answered any of the questions which tormented me. They filled me only with boredom; never with the feeling that they were communicating some verifiable power. I thought it useless, moreover, to speculate about abstractions without first defining them. And yet can one do otherwise? The only hope for a philosophy is to render itself impersonal. We must await this great step toward the time of the world's end.

I had dipped into a few mystics. It is impossible to speak ill of their works, for all one discovers there is what one brings.

I was at this point when *Eureka* fell into my hands.

124

My studies under my dull and woebegone professors had led me to believe that science is not love; that its fruits are perhaps useful, but its foliage very spiny and its bark terribly rough. I reserved mathematics for a type of boringly exact minds, incommensurable with my own.

Literature, on the other hand, had often shocked me by its lack of discipline, connexion, and necessity in handling ideas. Frequently its object is trifling. French poetry ignores, or even fears, all the tragedies and epics of the intellect. On the few occasions when it ventures into this territory, it becomes sad and dull beyond measure. Neither Lucretius nor Dante was French. We have no poets of the intelligence. Perhaps our feeling for the separation of literary *genres*—in other words, for the independence of the different movements of the mind—is such that we can suffer nothing which combines them. Those things which can exist without singing we cannot endow with song. But our poetry, during the last hundred years, has shown such a rare power of renewal that perhaps the future will not be slow to grant it some of those works which are grand in their style, noble in their severity, and dominate both the senses and the intellect.

In a few moments *Eureka* had introduced me to Newton's law, the name of Laplace, the hypothesis which he proposed, and the very existence of speculations and researches which were never mentioned to adolescents—for fear, I suppose, that we might be interested, instead of measuring the astonishing length of the hour with yawns and dreams. In those days, whatever was likely to stimulate the intellectual appetite was placed among the arcana. It was a time when fat textbooks of physics did not whisper a word about the law of gravity, or Carnot's principle, or the conservation of energy; instead they were addicted to Magdeburg hemispheres, three-branched faucets, and the tenuous theories to which they were laboriously inspired by the problem of the siphon.

And yet, would it be wasting the time of study to make young minds suspect the origins, high destinies, and living virtue of those computations and very arid theorems which pedagogues inflict on them without logical order, and even with a rather remarkable incoherence?

These sciences now taught so coldly were

founded and developed by men with a passionate interest in their work. *Eureka* made me feel some of this passion.

I confess that I was greatly astonished and only partially pleased by the preposterous claims and ambitions of the author, the solemn tone of his preamble, and the extraordinary discussion of method with which the volume opens. These first pages, however, gave indication of a central idea, although it was enveloped in a mystery which suggested partly a certain powerlessness, partly a deliberate reserve, and partly the reluctance of an enthusiastic soul to reveal its most precious secrets. . . . And all this did not leave me cold.

To attain what he calls *the truth*, Poe invokes what he calls *consistency*. It is not easy to give an exact definition of this consistency. The author has not done so, although he must have had a clear conception of its meaning.

According to him, the *truth* which he seeks can only be grasped by immediate adherence to an intuition of such nature that it renders present, and in some sort perceptible to the mind, the reciprocal dependence of the parts and properties of the system under consideration. This reciprocal dependence extends to the successive phases of the system; causality becomes symmetrical. To a point of view which embraced the totality of the universe, a cause and its effect might be taken one for the other; they could be said to exchange their rôles.

Two remarks at this point. The first I shall merely indicate, for it would lead us far, both the reader and myself. The doctrine of final causes plays a capital part in Poe's system. This doctrine is no longer fashionable, and I have neither the strength nor the desire to defend it. But we must agree that the notions of cause and adaptation lead almost inevitably to this conclusion (and I do not speak of the immense difficulties, and hence of the temptations, offered by certain facts, such as the existence of instincts, etc.) The simplest course is to dismiss the problem. Our only way of solving it is through pure imagination, and this can better be applied to other tasks.

Let us pass to the second remark. In Poe's system, consistency is both the source of the discovery and the discovery itself. This is an admirable conception: an example and application of reciprocal adaptation. The universe is formed on a plan the profound symmetry of which is present, as it were, in the inner structure of our minds. Hence, the poetic instinct will lead us blindly to the truth.

One frequently meets with analogous ideas among the mathematicians. They come to regard their discoveries not as "creations" of their mathematical faculties, but rather as something captured from a treasure composed of pre-existent and natural forms, a treasure which becomes accessible only through a rare conjecture of disciplined effort, sensibility, and desire.

All the consequences developed in *Eureka* are not deduced with the exactness, nor led up to with the degree of clarity, which one might desire. There are shadows and lacunæ. There are interventions which the author hardly explains. There is a God.

For the spectator of the dramas and comedies of the intellect, nothing is more interesting than to see the ingenuity, the insistency, the trickery and anxiety of an inventor at grips with his own invention. He is admirably familiar with all its defects. He inevitably wishes to display all its beauties, exploit its advantages, conceal its poverty, and at any cost make it the image of his ideal. A merchant adorns his merchandise. A woman changes her appearance before a mirror. Preachers, philosophers, politicians, and, in general, all men whose function is to expound uncertain things, are always a mixture of sincerity and silences (and this is the most favourable assumption). What they do not wish to consider, they do not wish us to see. . . .

The fundamental idea of *Eureka* is none the less a profound and sovereign idea.

It would not be exaggerating its importance to recognize, in his theory of consistency, a fairly definite attempt to describe the universe by its *intrinsic properties*. The following proposition can be found toward the end of *Eureka*: "Each law of nature depends at all points on all the other laws." This might easily be considered, if not as a formula, at least as the expression of a tendency toward generalized relativity.

That this tendency approaches recent conceptions becomes evident when one discovers, in the *poem* under discussion, an affirmation of the *symmetrical* and reciprocal relationship of matter, time, space, gravity, and light. I emphasize the word symmetrical, for *it is, in reality, a formal symmetry which is the essential characteristic of Einstein's universe.* Herein lies the beauty of his conception.

But Poe does not confine himself to the physical constituents of phenomena. He introduces life and consciousness into his plan. At this point how many thoughts occur to the mind! The time is past when one could distinguish easily between the material and the spiritual. Formerly all discussion was based on a complete knowledge of "matter," which it was thought could be limited by definition. In a word, everything depended on *appearance*.

The appearance of matter is that of a dead substance, a *potentiality* which becomes *activity* only through the intervention of something exterior and entirely foreign to its nature. From this definition, inevitable consequences used to be drawn. But matter has changed. Our old conception of its nature was derived from pure observation; experiments have led to an opposite notion. The whole of modern physics, which has created, as it were, *relays* for our senses, has persuaded us that our former definition had neither an absolute nor a speculative value. We find that matter is strangely diverse and infinitely surprising; that it is formed of transformations which continue and are lost in minuteness, even in the abysses of minuteness; we learn that perpetual motion is perhaps realized. In matter an eternal fever rages.

At present we no longer know what a fragment of any given body may or may not contain or produce, now or in the future. The very idea of matter is distinguished as little as you will from that of energy. Everything is stirred by deeper and deeper agitations, rotations, exchanges, radiations. Our own eyes, our hands, our nerves, are made of such stuff; and the appearance of death or sleep which matter at first presents, as well as its passivity and surrender to external forces, are conceptions built up in our senses, like those shadows obtained by a certain superposition of lights.

All this can be resumed in the statement that the properties of matter seem to depend only on the category of size in which we place the observer. But in this case the classical attributes of matter —its lack of spontaneity, its essential difference from movement, and the continuity or homogeneity of its texture—become merely superficial, and can no longer be absolutely contrasted with such concepts as life, sensibility, or thought. Once we depart from the category of size in which rough observations are made, all former definitions prove incorrect. We are certain that unknown properties and forces are exerted in the *infra-world,* since we have discovered a few of these which our senses were not made to perceive. But we can neither enumerate them, nor even assign a definite number to the increasing plurality of chapters in the science of physics.

We cannot even be certain that the whole body of our concepts is not illusory, when transported into those domains which limit and support our own. To speak of iron or hydrogen is to presuppose entities—the existence and permanence of which can only be inferred from very limited and comparatively brief experiments. Moreover, there is no reason to believe that our space, our time, and our causality preserve any meaning whatsoever in those domains where the existence of our bodies is *impossible.* And certainly, the man who attempts to imagine the inner reality of things can do so only by adapting the ordinary categories of his mind. But the more he extends his researches, and, in some degree, the more he increases his powers of recording phenomena, the further he travels from what might be called the *optimum* of his perceptions. Determinism is lost among inextricable systems, with billions of variables, where the mind's eye can no longer trace the operation of laws and come to rest on some permanent fact. Whereas the imagination was once employed in giving final form to a truth which the senses had led one to infer, and the power of logic had woven into a single piece—now, when discontinuity becomes the rule, this imagination must confess its impotence. And when the *means* become the objects of our judgments, we are ceasing to consider events in themselves. Our knowledge is tending toward power, and has turned aside from a co-ordinated contemplation of things; prodigies of mathematical subtlety are required to restore a little unity to our world. We mention first principles no longer, and physical laws have become mere instruments, always capable of being perfected. They no longer govern the world, but are involved in the weakness of our minds; we can no longer rely on their simplicity; always, like a persistent point, there is some unresolved decimal which brings us back to a feeling of incompleteness, a sense of the inexhaustible.

One can see, from these remarks, that Poe's intuitions as to the general nature of the physical, moral, and metaphysical universe are neither proved nor disproved by the extremely numerous and important discoveries which have been made since 1847. Certain of his views could even be incorporated, without excessive difficulty, into fairly recent conceptions. When he measures the duration of his Cosmos by the time necessary to realize all possible combinations of the elements, one thinks of Boltzmann's theories and of his estimates of probability as applied to the kinetic theory of gas. Carnot's principle is also foreshadowed in *Eureka*, as is the representation of this principle by the mechanics of diffusion; the author seems to have been a precursor of those bold spirits who would rescue the universe from its certain death by means of an infinitely brief passage through an infinitely improbable state.

Since a complete analysis of *Eureka* is not my present intention, I shall hardly mention the use which Poe makes of the nebular hypothesis. When

Laplace advanced this theory, his object was limited. He proposed only to reconstruct the development of the solar system. To this end he assumed the existence of a gaseous mass in the process of cooling. The core of the mass had already reached a high degree of condensation, and the whole rotated on an axis passing through its centre of gravity. He assumed the existence of this gravity, as well as the invariability of mechanical laws, and made it his sole task to explain the direction of rotation of the planets and their satellites, the slight eccentricity of their orbits, and the relatively small degree of inclination. Under these conditions, being subjected to centrifugal force and the process of cooling, matter would flow from the poles toward the equator of the mass, and at the points where gravity and centrifugal acceleration balanced each other, would be disposed in a zone. Thus a nebulous ring was formed; it would soon be broken, and the fragments of this ring would finally coalesce to form a planet.

The reader of *Eureka* will see how Poe has extended the application both of the nebular hypothesis and the law of gravity. On these mathematical foundations he has built an abstract poem, one of the rare modern examples of a total explanation of the material and spiritual universe, a *cosmogony*. It belongs to a department of literature remarkable for its persistence and astonishing in its variety; cosmogony is one of the oldest of all literary forms.

One might say that the world is hardly more ancient than the art of making the world. With a little more knowledge and much more intelligence, we might employ these Books of Genesis, whether taken from India, China, or Chaldea, whether belonging to Greece, Moses, or Svante Arrhenius, as standards to measure the spiritual simplicity of their own epochs. We should find, beyond doubt, that the naïvety of their aim is constant, but we should have to confess that its manifestations are exceedingly diverse.

Just as tragedy borders on history and psychology, the cosmogonic form verges sometimes on religion, with which it is confused at many points, and sometimes on science, from which it is necessarily distinguished by the absence of experimental proof. It includes sacred books, admirable poems, outlandish narratives full of beauties and absurdities, and physico-mathematical researches often so profound as to be worthy of a less insignificant subject than the universe. But it is the glory of man, and something more than his glory, to waste his powers on the void. Often these crack-brained researches are the cause of unexpected discoveries. The rôle of the non-existent exists; the function of the imaginary is real; and we learn from strict logic that *the false implies the true*. Thus it would seem that the history of thought can be summarized in these words: *It is absurd by what it seeks; great by what it finds*.

Both the problem of the totality of things and that of the origin of this totality arise from a very simple state of mind. We want to know what came before light; or perhaps we test some particular combination of ideas, to see whether it might not be placed before all others—whether it might not be considered as giving birth to the system which is the source of all our ideas—this system being the world; and to the author of all our ideas —this author being ourselves.

Whether we dream of an infinitely imperious Voice breaking, as it were, eternity; its first cry announcing Space, like tidings which grow ever more pregnant with consequence as they are carried toward the furthermost limits of the creative will; and the divine Word giving a place to essences, to life, to liberty, to the fatal contest between law and intelligence, between law and chance—or whether (if we hesitate to launch ourselves from pure nothingness toward any imaginable state) we find that the first epoch of the world is a little easier to consider in the vague idea of a mixture of matter and energy, composing a sort of substantial, but neutral and powerless mud, which patiently awaits the act of a demiurge—or finally whether, more profound, better equipped, but no less thirsty for marvels, we invoke the aid of all the sciences to reconstruct the earliest possible condition of the system which is the object of every science—in any case our idea of the origin of things is never more than a reverie based on their present disposition; it is in some sort a degeneration of the real, a variation on what is.

What do we actually need before we can think of this origin?

If we need the idea of nothingness, the idea of nothingness is nothing; or rather, it is already something; it is a pretence of the mind, which plays a comedy of silence and perfect shadows; in the midst of these shadows I am sure that I lie hidden and am ready to create, simply by relaxing my attention; I feel myself to be present, and indispensable, and endowed with will, so that I may preserve, by a conscious act, this ephemeral absence of all images and this apparent nullity. . . . But it is an image and it is an act; I call myself *Nothingness* by a momentary convention.

Or, if the idea which I place at the origin of all things is that of an extreme disorder, extending to the smallest particles of existence, I can easily perceive that this inconceivable chaos is ordered by my purpose of conception. I jumbled the cards myself, for the joy of arranging them later. And besides, to define a disorder so confused that one could neither discover the slightest trace of order nor substitute another chaos more thorough and more advanced, would be a masterpiece of art and logic. A confusion which truly lies at the beginning of things must be an infinite confusion. But in this case we cannot derive the world from it, and the very perfection of this chaos renders its use forever impossible.

As for the idea of a beginning—I mean an absolute beginning—it is necessarily a myth. Every beginning is a coincidence: we must imagine it as some sort of contact between all and nothing. In trying to think of it, we find that every beginning is a consequence—every beginning *ends* something.

But principally we need the idea of this Whole we call the *universe*, the beginning of which we desire to know. Even before we commence to puzzle over the problem of its origin, let us see whether the very notion of a universe, which seems to impose itself on our minds, and which we find so simple and inevitable, will not disintegrate under our eyes.

We imagine vaguely that the *Whole* is *something*, and imagining *something*, we call it the *Whole*. We believe that it began as all things begin, and that this beginning of the Whole, which must have been far more strange and impressive than that of the parts, must also be infinitely more important to know. We form an idol of totality, and an idol of its origin, and are drawn to conclude the reality of a certain body of nature, whose unity corresponds to another unity of which we are firmly convinced—that of ourselves.

Such is the primitive, almost the childish, form

of our idea of the universe. It is very natural; in other words very impure. We must examine it more closely, and ask ourselves whether this notion can form a part of any but a fallacious chain of reason.

I shall observe in myself what I think under this head.

A rudimentary universe is offered by all the things I see, considered as a whole. My eyes conduct my vision from place to place, and everywhere find impressions. My vision, by stimulating the mobility of my eyes, is increased, broadened, and deepened continually. There is no movement of the eyes which encounters a region of invisibility; there is none which does not give rise to effects of colour. By these movements, which are prolonged and mutually connected, which absorb or correspond to one another, I am as if enclosed in my power of vision. All my different perceptions are harmonized and arranged in the unity of my directing consciousness.

I acquire the general and constant impression that a sphere of simultaneity is attached to my presence. It moves along with me, and its contents are infinitely variable; but through all the substitutions it may undergo, it preserves its fullness. I may change my place, or the bodies which surround me may be modified, but the unity of my total representation, and the property it has of surrounding me, are in no wise altered. It is vain to flee or attempt in any manner to escape; I am always enveloped by all the *seeing-movements* of my body, which are transformed one into another, and inevitably carry me back to the same central situation.

Thus I see a *whole*. I regard it as a Whole, because it might be said to exhaust my capacity for seeing. My vision is confined to this closed circle, and to the juxtaposition which surrounds me. All my other sensations have reference to some spot within this circle, of which the centre thinks and speaks.

Such is my first Universe. I do not know whether a man blind from birth could have so clear and immediate notion of a sum of all things, for I am convinced that the particular properties of vision are essential to the formation, *by myself*, of an entire and complete domain. Sight in some sort assumes the function of simultaneity—in other words, of unity as such.

But the unity which is necessarily formed of everything I can see in an instant—this mass of figures or blotches reciprocally joined, from which I later disentangle matter, depth, movement, and events, giving a place to each—this whole which I observe in order to discover what attracts and what alarms me—it is this which inspires me with the first idea, the model and, as it were, the germ of the total universe which I believe to exist around my sensation, masked and revealed by it. Inevitably I imagine that an immense and hidden system supports, penetrates, nourishes, and reabsorbs every actual and sensible element of my duration, forcing it to exist and to be resolved; and that hence every moment is formed of an infinite number of roots that plunge to an unknown depth in an *implicit space*—in the past—in the secret structure of this our machine for perceiving and combining, which returns incessantly to the *present*. The present, considered as a permanent relationship of all the changes which touch me, suggests the image of a solid to which all my perceptive life is attached, like a sea-anemone to its bit of shingle. On this stone, this pebble, how can I build an edifice outside of which nothing could exist? How can I pass from a limited and instantaneous universe to one which is complete and absolute?

It would now be a question of conceiving and constructing, around a real germ, a figure which must satisfy two essential conditions: first, that it should admit all things, be capable of all things, and represent all things to us; secondly, that it serve our intelligence, lend itself to our reasonings, and render us, to a little higher degree, the lords of knowledge and masters of ourselves.

But merely to specify these two necessities of the intellect, merely to set them side by side, is enough to waken sharply all the insurmountable difficulties which reside in the slightest attempt to give a workable definition of the Universe.

Universe, therefore, is only a mythological expression. The thoughts suggested by this word are perfectly irregular and entirely independent. As soon as we leave the bounds of the moment, as soon as we attempt to enlarge and extend our presence outside of itself, our forces are exhausted in our liberty. We are surrounded by all the disorder of our knowledge, of our faculties. We are beseiged by all that is memory, all that is possible, all that is imaginable, all that is calculable, all the combinations of our spirit in all degrees of probability, in all states of precision. How can we form a concept of something which is opposed to nothing, rejects nothing, resembles nothing? If it resembled something, it would no longer be the whole. If it resembles nothing. . . . And, if this totality is equivalent in power to our mind, our mind has no hold over it. All the objections which are raised against an active infinity, all the difficulties which arise when one attempts to draw order out of multiplicity, are here involved. No proposition can be advanced about this *subject* so disordered in its richness that all *attributes* apply to it. Just as the universe escapes our intuition, in the same way it is transcendent to our logic.

And as for its origin—*in the beginning was fable.* There it will always remain.

VARIATIONS ON A THEME
FROM PASCAL

VARIATIONS ON A THEME
FROM PASCAL

The eternal silence. . . .

"What are the soft, imperious sounds," Eusta-
thius asks Pythagoras, "and what strangely pure
harmonies are those I seem to hear in the substance
of the night which wraps us round? My soul, on
the furthermost bounds of hearing, is startled by
the echo of distant modulations. It reaches out,
like hope, to the very limit of the senses, straining
to hear those crystal shivers, those slow, majestic
sighs which nourish me with marvels. What, O
Pythagoras, is the mysterious instrument of these
delights?"

"The heavens themselves," Pythagoras replied.
"You are hearing the music which charms the gods.
There is no silence in the universe. A concert of
eternal voices is inseparable from the movement
of the celestial bodies. Each of these revolving
stars, according to its speed, sets up vibrations in
the ether and fills all space with the sound proper

to its number. The farther planets, which are necessarily more rapid, furnish the shriller notes to the chorus; those nearer to us, moving more slowly, emit more solemn tones, and the motionless earth is dumb. Since the spheres are subject to law, the sounds they engender are united in a sweet and sweetly variable harmony, which is that of the skies with the skies. It is the order of the pure world which enchants your ears. Intelligence, justice, love and the other perfections which reign in the sublime part of the universe are made audible; and the extreme delight you feel is only the effect of a divine and rigorous analogy. . . .

So it was that the profound desire of the ancient Greeks peopled the abysses of the night.

As for the Jews, they never spoke of the skies without celebrating their eloquence. The biblical night resound in praises of the Lord. The heavenly bodies are sometimes confused with the sons of God, who are the angels, and this innumerable tribe of spirits and stars bursts forth in immense acclamation; their voices are heard through all the earth.

"The heavens declare the glory of God; and the firmament sheweth his handywork."

The author of the Psalms finds no terms of sufficient vigour to express all the power of this extraordinary voice: "Day unto day uttereth speech, and night unto night sheweth knowledge. There is no speech nor language where their voice is not heard. Their line is gone out through all the earth, and their words to the end of the world . . . *Non sunt loquelae neque sermones quorum non audiantur voces eorum. In omnem terram exivit sonus eorum et in fines orbis terrae verba eorum.*"

And Jehovah himself says to Job: "The morning stars sang together, and all the sons of God shouted for joy."

From the infinite spaces, Pascal receives only silence. He speaks of himself as "terrified." He complains with bitterness of being abandoned in the world. Nowhere does he discover the traces of Him who declared by the mouth of Jeremiah, "*Coelum et terram ego impleo,* I fill the heavens and the earth." And this strange Christian cannot find his Father in the skies. But, on the contrary, "as he regards all the speechless universe, he is filled with terror, like a man carried in his sleep to a desert and terrible isle."

Terror, terrified, terrible; eternal silence; speech-less universe—such is the fashion in which one of the keenest intellects that ever existed speaks of the world surrounding it.

Pascal suffers and depicts his sufferings; he wails like a hunted beast, but also like a beast that hunts itself. He draws on his own great resources, the wealth of his logic, the admirable virtues of his style, to corrupt everything visible which is not desolating. He wishes himself to be fragile and completely menaced, and surrounded on every side by perils and solitude, and all the causes of terror and despair. He cannot bear to think that he has been taken in the nets of time, of number, of dimension; nor that he has been snared by the system of the world. There is no created thing which does not remind him of his fearful condition; some wound him, others deceive, and all horrify, to such a degree that meditation on these subjects never fails to send him into mortal groans. Inevitably he makes me think of the intolerable howls which dogs address to the moon; but this despairing wretch, who is capable of formulating a theory of the moon, howls with equal desperation against his own theories.

It is not only what takes place in the sky, but everything; and not only everything in itself, but even the innocent representation of things, which he finds hateful and exasperating: "What vanity is painting. . . ." He invents, for the images which are the objects of the arts, a sort of secondary disdain.

I cannot help thinking that there must be system and method in this attitude of perfect melancholy and this absolute degree of disgust. A well-turned phrase excludes the idea of total renunciation.

A despair which writes well is not so thorough as to have salvaged no liberty of thought from the shipwreck of its hopes. It has a sense of rhythm, a logic, and a feeling for symbols which, by their existence, contradict what they say. Besides, there is something ambiguous and something facile in this specialized choice of tragic themes and awe-inspiring objects. What do we teach other men by repeating that they are nothing, that life is vain, that nature is hostile and knowledge an illusion? What virtue in confounding the nothing which they are, and why reiterate what they know already?

I never feel easy before this mixture of art and nature. When I see an author describing and maligning the real sensations of man, adding studied effects, and asking in spite of all that we take his industry for his emotion, I find his work ambiguous and impure. This confusion of the true and the false becomes very offensive when we suspect the author of trying to change our convictions or impart a tendency. If you wish to convince or surprise me, take care lest I see your hand more clearly than the lines it traces.

The hand of Pascal is too visible.

And besides, even where the intentions are honest, the mere effort of composition, and the care one devotes to it, have the same effect as a studied insincerity. It is inevitable that one should render extreme that which was moderate, and dense that which was rare, and more entire that which was in parts, and pathetic that which was merely animated. . . . The false windows draw themselves in. The artist can scarcely refrain from intensifying his original impression; and he renders the de-

154

velopments of his original idea symmetrical, almost in the same way that the nervous system generalizes some local modification and extends it over the whole body. This is not an objection to the artist as such, but a warning never to confuse the real man who composed the work with the imaginary author that the work leads one to infer.

In the case of Pascal, this confusion is the general rule. So much has been written about him; he has been so often pictured and so passionately considered, that he has become a character of tragedy; a curious actor, almost a stock type of the comedy of knowledge. Certain men play the Pascal. Convention has made him a sort of French and Jansenist Hamlet. Holding his own skull in his hands, the skull of a great mathematician, he trembles and dreams on a platform facing the universe instead of Elsinore. He is seized by the harsh winds of infinity; he delivers monologues on the brink of the abyss, exactly as from the boards of a theatre; and he argues, before the whole world, with the ghost of himself.

However, it is a rather extraordinary fact that most religions have placed the throne of the Almighty at an extreme height; and have found his token and the proofs of his existence in that sidereal order which, on the other hand, gave men the idea, the primitive model, and the first demonstration of natural laws.

It is toward the sky that hands are stretched; in the sky that eyes take refuge or are lost; to the sky that prophets or redeemers point; from the height of heaven that certain words once fell, and certain blasts of trumpets were made heard.

Doubtless the First Cause, the Pure Act, and the Spirit have no abode, just as they have neither form nor parts; but an instinct which derives, perhaps, from our vertical structure; or perhaps the feeling that our destiny is linked with remote phenomena, and that all terrestrial life depends on these, has caused the race of man, when troubled or afflicted, or tormented in their minds by violent doubts, to turn inevitably toward the zenith of the place, to *lift their eyes on high*.

Kant himself, yielding to a secret impulse of naïve mysticism, conjoined the sort of inspiration he had of a universal moral law with the feeling he derived from the spectacle of the starry sky.

Being impressed by the mysterious mood induced in most men by a pure night and the presence of stars, I have sometimes tried to observe it in myself, and define the ideas to which it gives rise.

At such times the only objects we perceive are those which have nothing to do with our bodies. We are strangely simplified. Everything near is invisible; everything visible is intangible. We wander far from ourselves. Our attention is wholly claimed by vision, and confined to a field of luminous events which it cannot refrain from uniting one with the other by its own spontaneous movements, as if they existed on the same plane. It traces lines and forms figures which belong only to our attention; these it imposes upon us and introduces into the real spectacle.

However, we cannot arrange and distribute all these points. We are overwhelmed, bombarded, swallowed up, neglected by this numerous twinkling.

We can count the stars, and yet are unable to believe that we exist for them. Between the stars and us, there is no reciprocity.

We are conscious of something which demands speech, and something else which forbids it.

Since what we see in the sky and what we find in the depth of ourselves are equally independent of our actions, one of them gleaming beyond our enterprise and the other existing beneath our level of expression, a sort of relation is formed between the attention we devote to the most remote phenomena and that we devote to the most subjective things. These two sorts of attention are, as it were, the poles of our expectancy—extremes which correspond, and even resemble each other by virtue of our hope for some decisive event, either in the heavens or in the heart.

To this army of stars, so prodigious in our sight, the inner being opposes a desperate feeling of being itself, of being unique—and yet of being alone. I am the whole, and incomplete. I am the whole and a part.

The darkness which surrounds us lays bare our souls.

This darkness is strewn with inaccessible gleams. We can hardly avoid thinking of homes where some one wakes. Vaguely we people the shadows with luminous, unknowable beings.

The same darkness which veils our immediate surroundings, correspondingly dulls the sound of our words, reducing them to an interior voice; for we tend to hold real speech only with those near by.

We feel a singular calm, a singular discomfort. There is no longer any bridge between the ego and the non-ego. As long as daylight lasted, there had been a connexion between our thoughts and external things, by means of our acts. We traded sensations for thoughts, and thoughts for sensations; our acts served as intermediaries, our time as money. But at present there is no more trading. The man of action, who is the measure of all things, has ceased to exist. Nothing exists save two distinct presences, two incommensurable natures. There are only two adversaries who watch each other and do not understand. The enormous extension of our perspectives is confronted with the diminution of our power; and for a time we lose the familiar illusion that external things correspond to us. We are like flies on a window through which they cannot pass.

It is impossible for us to remain in this dormant state. The sensibility is a stranger to equilibrium. It might even be defined as a function which exists to destroy, in living creatures, all equilibrium of their faculties. Inevitably the mind will be roused, will struggle out of its stupor and recover from the solemn and motionless surprise which was caused by the feeling of our being all, and the evidence of our being nothing.

And now one sees that hermit by essence, the mind, defending itself with its thoughts. Our body, for defence against the world, employs its reflexes and glandular secretions; sometimes it produces them at hazard, as if to do something hastily, while sometimes opportune movements and effective humours are accurately opposed to the condition of oppression or irritation. The soul is hardly different in its reaction to the inhumanity of the night. It defends itself by means of its own creations, some of which are as simple and irrepressible as reflexes, while others are deliberate, delayed, combined, articulated, and adapted to our understanding of the situation.

Hence we shall find in ourselves two types of response to the sensation I ascribed to our regarding the sky and imagining the universe. Some of our reactions will be *spontaneous,* and others *elaborated*. Their natures are very different, although they can be mingled and combined in the same brain; but they must be separated to be defined.

They are often distinguished by attributing the former to the *heart*, the latter to the *mind*. These terms will serve our purpose.

The heart, in its struggle against the terrifying figure of the world, nearly always arrives, by force of desire, at the idea of some Being powerful enough to contain, to have formed, or to emit that monstrous mass of space and radiations which produces, nourishes, and surrounds us; which menaces, fascinates, puzzles, and finally devours us. And this Being may even be a Person—bearing, in other words, some likeness to ourselves, and offering an indefinite hope of an indefinable union. This is what the heart *finds*. It tends to answer itself with a god.

We have learned, moreover, from the experience of love that the unique has need of the unique; that whoever lives desires the living.

Let us now see what other type of thoughts will occur to us if we defer our sentiment, and try to oppose an infinite patience and immense interest to the enormous pressure of all things. The mind *seeks*.

The mind will not hasten to imagine a defence against the stare of the universe. It will examine

—without regard to time, or the length of a particular life. There is a remarkable contrast between the quickness, eagerness, anxiety of the "heart," and this patience formed of criticism and hope. The delay, which may be limitless, has the effect of transforming the problem; and the transformation of the search may transform the seeker.

We shall discover that we cannot think of our universe except by conceiving it as an *object* clearly separable from ourselves, and distinctly opposed to our consciousness. We shall then be able to compare it with such little systems as we are able to describe, define, experiment with, and measure. We shall treat the whole as a part. We shall be led to consider the universe under the terms of a logic whose operations will allow us to predict cosmic changes, or to limit their domain.

(For example, we shall compare all the stars to a gaseous cloud, we shall apply the laws discovered by studying gases in the laboratory to a swarm of stars, we shall form a "statistical" idea of the universe, we shall think of its "internal energy," of its "temperature," etc.)

Briefly, our task will consist in comparing that which was so stupefying, so prodigal of emotion, with that which is familiar to our senses, accessible to our actions, and in fairly close agreement with our thoughts.

But from all this limitless labour there results —there must necessarily result in the course of time—a certain variation (already perceptible) of that *familiar*, that *possible*, and that *reasonable* which will always be the requisites of our content. Just as men have accepted the antipodes, they will become familiar with the "curvature of the universe" and many other novelties. It is not impossible—it is even fairly probable—that such familiarity will little by little transform not only our ideas, but many of our immediate reactions.

What might be called the "reaction of Pascal" may become a rarity and an object of curiosity to psychologists.

Pascal had "found," but doubtless only because he no longer sought. A cessation of research, and the form of that cessation, may give the feeling of discovery.

But he never had faith in research, in so far as it hopes for the unexpected.

Out of himself he derived the *eternal silence*

163

which neither truly religious nor truly profound men have ever observed in the universe.

Appallingly, grossly, he exaggerated the hostility between science and salvation; for learned men could be found in the same century who were no less worthy of salvation, I believe, than Pascal himself, but who did not allow the sciences to suffer for that cause. There was Cavalieri, with his studies of indivisibles; there was Saccheri, who suspected, without directly acknowledging, the part which mere assumption plays in Euclid, and thereby opened a road for the daring explorations of many future mathematicians. These men, it is true, were only Jesuits.

A TRIBUTE

A TRIBUTE

A TRIBUTE

ALTHOUGH I have read only one volume of Marcel Proust's great work, and that volume none too well; although to me the very art of the novel is an almost inconceivable art; still, from the few chapters of *Remembrance of Things Past* which I had opportunity to read, I can realize the exceptional loss which has lately been suffered by Letters; and not by them alone, but even more by that secret order or society which consists, at any period, of those readers who give letters their true value.

And even if I had not read a single line of this vast work, but had only found the generally so discordant minds of André Gide and Léon Daudet agreed on its importance, this would have been enough to insure me against doubt; such a rare encounter could only take place somewhere in the neighbourhood of certainty. We can be sure that the sun is shining if both of them say so at once.

Others will speak in profound and accurate terms of a work so moving and subtle. Still others will describe the character of the man who conceived it and developed it so gloriously; for my part I had only a glimpse of him, and that was years ago. All I can offer here is an opinion which lacks the force of knowledge, and is almost unworthy to be written. It will merely be a tribute, a perishable flower on an enduring tomb.

Every literary form being based on some particular use of language, the novel employs the immediate and significative power of words in order to communicate one or several imaginary "lives." It fixes the time and place of these, chooses the characters, and lists the incidents, which it connects by a more or less sufficient shadow of causation.

Whereas poetry affects our organism directly, and tends toward song, which is an exact and continuous exercise of co-operation between hearing, the form of the voice, and articulate expression—the novel endeavours to excite and sustain in us that general and irregular expectancy which is our attitude toward real events; their strange causation or their ordinary sequence is imitated by the story-teller's art. And whereas the world of poetry is essentially closed and complete in itself, being purely the system of the ornaments and accidents of language, the universe of the novel, even of the fantastic novel, is joined to the real world—just as the painted background of a window-display merges imperceptibly into real objects, among which a spectator comes and goes.

The appearance of "life" and "truth," which is the object of the novelist's plans and ambitions, depends on the continual introduction of *observations*—in other words, of identifiable elements, which he incorporates into his plan. A web of true or imagined details unites the real existence of the reader with the pretended existence of the characters; whence it results that these shadows often acquire a strange power of life, and are mingled in our thoughts with actual people. Unconsciously we lend them all the human lives which exist in us potentially, for our faculty of living implies that of giving life. As much as we lend them, so much is the novel worth.

There need be no essential difference between a novel and a natural account of things we have seen and heard. No rhythms, symmetries, figures, or forms are imposed on the novelist, nor even a definite form of composition. There is only one law, but that is enforced on pain of death. It is required

—and it suffices—that the story should carry and even *inspire* us toward some goal, which may be the illusion of having lived violently or profoundly through an adventure, or may be that of having gained complete knowledge of invented characters. It is remarkable—and could easily be proved by the example of popular novels—that a collection of details which are insignificant in themselves, and valueless one by one (since they can be transformed one by one into others of equal facility), should produce a passionate interest and the effect of life.—From this we should draw no conclusions against the novel; at the most we might find some degree of blame against life, which is the perfectly real sum of things, part of which are vain, the others imaginary.

It follows that the novel can admit everything which is suggested and admitted by any orderly development of our memory, when it recalls and comments upon a period through which we lived—not only portraits, landscapes, and what is called "psychology," but in addition all sorts of thoughts, and allusions to all forms of knowledge. It can affect and convince all of the mind.

In this respect the novel definitely approaches

the state of dreams. Both can be defined by considering this curious property: *that all their digressions are strictly part of them.*

Generally it is poetry which people associate with dreams, and I find this notion superficial.

Unlike poems, a novel can be *summarized;* in other words its own plot can be *told;* it can be shortened without materially changing the story; thus it contains a part which can, if desired, be made implicit. A novel can also be *translated* without losing its value. It can be *developed* internally or *prolonged* indefinitely, and it can be read in several sittings. The only bounds to its length and diversity are those which limit the forces and leisure of the reader; and all the restrictions which can be imposed on this form do not proceed from its own essence, but merely from the intentions and particular decisions of the writer.

These simple and broad conditions Proust has employed to extraordinary advantage. He did not give the impression of life forcibly, by pure action; rather he rejoined and in some sort imitated life, by the superabundance of associations which even the most fleeting images so easily found in the very substance of the author. He gave infinite roots to all the seeds of analysis which the circumstances of his life had sown in its duration. The interest of his works resides in each of their fragments. We can open the book to any page we choose; its vitality does not depend on what proceeds, or on the *acquired illusion;* it derives from what might be called the *activity proper* of the very tissue of his text.

What other writers are accustomed to pass over, Proust divides—and gives us the impression of being able to divide indefinitely.

We others neglect the resources on which he drew. At any given moment of our lives we have just failed to recognize an *infinity of power,* which might be defined as the property, common to all remembered impressions, of combining one with another. To advance in our careers, and be equal to events, we are forced to neglect that quality of imminence which exists in the depths of our nature. Our characters are shaped by an act which is performed, and is performed at the expense of all possible acts. By virtue of our consciousness, we are completely inexhaustible—we who cannot pause for a moment in ourselves without being immediately aware of innumerable thoughts; without seeing them changed one for the other, or rather developed from one into another, so as to open a perspective of parentheses. The soul must be always creating, and always devouring its creatures. Incessantly it is sketching the outline of other lives, giving birth to its heroes and monsters, blocking out theories, commencing poems. . . . There is a treasure of surpassing value and no value at all, from which each man of us derives the man he is; it is composed of all we lose, or think we lose, and of everything we can hope from ourselves; and it is this treasure, beyond a doubt, which Marcel Proust referred to as *the Past*. Until he appeared, no author, or almost none, had deliberately utilized its resources. It meant employing all of his being, and in this task his being was consumed.

Proust was able to adapt the potentialities of his inner life, which was singularly rich and curiously elaborated, to his aim of expressing one group of people, a little society which wished to be, and should be, *superficial*. By virtue of what he accomplished, the picture of a superficial society became a profound work.

Should so much thought be expended in such

a task? Was the object worthy of so much effort and an attention so long sustained? This question deserves careful examination.

The group which calls itself Society is composed only of symbolic figures. Each of its members represents some abstraction. It is necessary that all the powers of this world should somewhere meet together: that *money* should converse with *beauty*, and *politics* become familiar with *elegance;* that *letters* and *birth* grow friendly and serve each other tea. After a new power has gained recognition, no great time passes before its representatives appear at the gatherings of society; and the movement of history is pretty well summarized by the successive admission of different social types to the salons, hunts, marriages, and funerals of the supreme tribe of a nation.

Since all the abstractions I mentioned are represented by individuals who are what they are, contrasts and complications result which can only be observed on this narrow stage. Just as a banknote is only a slip of paper, so the member of society is a sort of fiduciary money made of living flesh. This combination is extremely favourable to the designs of a subtle novelist.

We must not forget that the greatest French writers have rarely treated anything but the Court. From Town, they drew only comedies; from Country, fables and nothing else. But very great art, which is the art of simplified figures and the most pure types; in other words, of essences which permit the symmetrical and almost musical development of the consequences arising from a carefully isolated situation—such art involves the existence of a conventional *milieu,* where the language is adorned with veils and provided with limits, where *seeming* commands *being,* and where *being* is held in a noble restraint which changes all of life into an opportunity to exercise presence of mind. . . .

The Society of our time is not so clearly organized as was the Court of days gone by. None the less, and perhaps by virtue of a certain disorder and the interesting contradictions to be observed, it is worthy of being used by the inventor of Charlus and the Guermantes as the source of his characters and pretexts, some of which are extremely delicate. In his personal depths, however, Marcel Proust sought for the metaphysics without which no society can exist.

As for his methods, they belong incontestably to our most admirable tradition. We sometimes find that his works are not very easy to read. But I am always ready to answer that we must be thankful for the difficult authors of our time. If they shape the minds of a few readers, it is not merely for their own use. By the same token they offer these readers to Montaigne, Descartes, Bossuet, and a few others who are still, perhaps, worth study. All these great men speak abstractly; they reason; they go deeply into their subject; with a single sentence they outline all the body of an elaborate thought. They do not fear the reader; they measure neither his labour nor their own. A few years more, and they will no longer be understood.

AN INTRODUCTION
TO THE METHOD OF
LEONARDO DA VINCI

I. *Note and Digression* (1919)
II. *Introduction* (1894)

I

NOTE AND DIGRESSION

(1919)

*And why, you will ask, did the author dispatch
his hero into Hungary?*

*Because he wished to include a piece of music
with a Hungarian theme. This he confesses
frankly. He would have sent the hero anywhere in
the world if he had found the slightest musical
reason for so doing.*

From the Foreword to *The Damnation of Faust,*
by Hector Berlioz.

I MUST apologize for choosing such an ambitious title, and one which in reality is so misleading. When I attached it to this brief study, I
had no intention of imposing on the reader. But
twenty-five years have passed since I placed it
there, and now, long after my ardour has cooled,
I find it more than a little pretentious. And so
it would be best to modify the title. As for the
text. . . . But I should not even dream of writing it today. *Impossible!* the reason would exclaim.

179

When the game of chess which he plays with knowledge has reached its nth move, a man begins to think that he is learning from his adversary; he assumes the manner of the latter, turns pitiless toward the young man he is forced to acknowledge as his ancestor, discovers inexplicable faults, which were the audacities of that young man, and reconstructs the naïvety of his own past. All of which is equivalent to making himself more stupid than he really was, but stupid by necessity, stupid for reasons of state! No temptation is keener or closer to the soul, and none, perhaps, is more fruitful, than that of denying oneself. Each day is jealous of the days, and such is its duty; the mind struggles desperately not to admit that it has ever been more capable; the clarity of any given moment refuses to illuminate past moments which were clearer than itself; and the first phrase which vibrates weakly, at the touch of the sun, through the awakening brain; the first sentence to go echoing through this Memnon is: "To reckon nothing accomplished, *nihil reputare actum.*"

To reread, therefore; to reread after having forgotten—to reread *oneself,* without a shadow of tenderness, without paternity; coldly and with critical acumen, and in a mood terribly conducive to ridicule and contempt; one's air hostile, one's eye destructive—is to recast one's work, or feel that it should be recast, into a very different mould.

Such an object is worth the effort, but has always been beyond my power. To tell the truth, I never dreamed of attempting it; this little essay owes its existence to Mme. Juliette Adam, who, toward the end of the year 1894, at the kind instance of M. Léon Daudet, asked me to write it for her journal, *La Nouvelle Revue*.

Even at twenty-three, I was immensely perplexed. I was only too well aware that I knew Leonardo a great deal less than I admired him. I regarded him as the principal character of that Intellectual Comedy which has not yet found its poet, and which in my judgment would be far more precious than the *Comédie Humaine*; more precious, even, than *The Divine Comedy*. I felt that this ruler of his own resources, this master of design, of symbols, and of calculations, had found the central attitude from which all the enterprises of learning or science and all the operations of art are equally possible, and a successful co-operation between analysis and action is singularly probable —a wonderfully stimulating thought.

But also too immediate—a thought without value, infinitely diffuse—a thought to be spoken, not to be written down.

I was charmed and overwhelmed by this Apollo. What could be more seductive than a god who despises mystery; who does not base his power on our agitated senses, nor cast his incantations over the darkest, most tender, most evil part of our nature; who forces our minds to agree, not to submit; whose miracle is to be lucid, and whose profundity is a well-devised perspective. Is there any surer sign of real and legitimate power than its not being exercised under a veil?—Never had Dionysus a more deliberate enemy, nor one so pure and so armed with light, as this hero who aimed less at bending and breaking monsters than examining their structure; who disdained to wound them with arrows because his questions went deeper; who was more their superior than their conqueror; who seemed to declare that the most effective triumph is to understand one's foes—almost to the point of reproducing them. Once having grasped their principle, he can abandon them in derision, reduced to their humble condition of very special cases and explainable paradoxes.

His drawings and manuscripts, little as I had studied them, had filled me with a sort of awe. From these thousands of notes and sketches, I gained the extraordinary impression of an hallucinating shower of sparks, torn by all sort of blows from some fantastic invention. Maxims, receipts, advice to himself, projects formed by a reason which corrects its own blunders, sometimes a finished description; sometimes he speaks to himself as if to a close friend. . . .

But I had no desire to repeat that he was this and that; not only a painter, but a mathematician and . . .

And, in a word, the artist of the world itself. No one is ignorant of the fact.

I was too little versed in the subject to dream of explaining his researches in detail—of trying, for example, to determine the exact meaning of that *impeto* which plays so great a part in his dynamics; or of discussing the *sfumato* which he

pursued in his painting. I was neither erudite nor
even inclined to be so, and hence could not think
of contributing anything whatever to the simple
multiplication of known facts. For erudition I
felt less fervour than it deserves. As I listened to
the astonishing conversation of Marcel Schwob,
I was more impressed by its charm than by its
sources. I drank in every word he said, and had
the pleasure of erudition without its pain. But
finally, I roused myself. All my laziness revolted
against the idea of the discouraging studies, the
endless collations, and the scrupulous methods
which serve only to keep us from certainty. I
told my friend that learned men run more risk
than others, because they lay wagers and we stay
out of the game; and because they have two ways
of deceiving themselves: our way, which is easy,
and their own, which is laborious. That even if
they have the good fortune to restore a few events,
the very number of material facts established in
this way is a danger to the reality which we are
seeking. Truth in the raw is more false than falsehood. From documents we derive a haphazard
mixture of rules and exceptions. Even a chron-
icler or diarist prefers to set down the peculiarities,

rather than the generally accepted customs, of his age.

Moreover, everything which is true of an age or a person does not always add to our real knowledge of one or the other. Nobody is equal to the exact total of his appearances; and is there any man who has never said, or has never done, something which was not *his*? Sometimes imitation, sometimes a lapse—or an occasion—or merely the accumulated boredom of being exactly what one is, of being oneself, distorts that very self for a moment. We are sketched during a dinner; the drawing is handed down to a posterity composed exclusively of scholars, and so we are prettified for the whole of literary eternity. A scowling face, if photographed at the instant of the scowl, is an irrefutable document. But show it to the friends of the victim, and they will fail to recognize the portrait.

My dislike of prolonged study was ingenious, and I had many other sophistries at the beck of my aversions. Nevertheless, I might perhaps have confronted these difficulties if only I believed they would lead me to the end which I loved. I loved, in my darkness, the inner law of the great Leo-

nardo. I was not interested in his biography, and
I would not be satisfied merely to know the creations of his thought. . . . Of this head that bowed
under many crowns, I dreamed only of grasping
the *essence*.

What was I to do, intoxicated as I was with intellectual cupidity and pride, but faced by so many
refutations and supported only by the wealth of
my desires?

Should I give rein to my enthusiasm?—Finally
manage to contract some literary fever? Culti-
vate its enthusiasm?

I longed for a glorious subject. How little this
signifies when one sits down to write!

A great thirst can doubtless refresh itself with
liquid visions; it acts on I do not know what secret
substances, and is like invisible light playing over
Bohemian glass which contains uranium; it illumi-
nates that which it desires; it imagines sparkling
pitchers, and depicts the opalescence of carafes.
. . . But the beverages it makes are only specious;
and I have always found it ignoble to write by
enthusiasm alone. Enthusiasm is not the state of
a writer's soul.

However great the energy of fire, it becomes useful and a motive force only by virtue of the machines in which it is confined by human skill. Well-placed restraints must prevent its total wastage, and some obstacle must be opposed to the inevitable return of equilibrium; otherwise we derive nothing from the futile dissipation of heat.

The same generality applies to literary composition. In this case, however, the author feels himself to be at once the *source* of energy, the *engineer* of the machine, and the *restraints*. One part of him is impulsion; another foresees, organizes, moderates, suppresses; a third (logic and memory) maintains the conditions, preserves the connexions, and assures some permanence to the desired combination. . . . *To write* should really mean to construct, as solidly and exactly as possible, a machine of language in which the force of the stimulated mind is used in overcoming *real* obstacles; hence the writer must be divided against himself. This is the sole respect in which, strictly speaking, the whole man acts as *author*. Everything else is not of *him*, but of a part of him, escaped. Between the emotion or initial intention and those final results which are disorder, vagueness, and forgetting—the fatal destinies of thought—it is his task to introduce the obstacles which he creates, so that being interposed, they may struggle with the purely transitory nature of psychic phenomena to win a measure of renewable action, a share of independent existence.

Perhaps in those days I exaggerated the evident defect of all literature, which is never to satisfy the whole of the mind. I did not like the idea of leaving some faculties idle while the others were being employed. I might also say (and it amounts to the same thing) that I placed nothing above *consciousness*; I would have given many master-pieces which I believed to be guided by impulse for one page visibly directed by the mind.

These errors would be easy to defend. I am not yet fully convinced of their being sterile, and even on some occasions return to them; still, they poisoned my efforts at that time. Not only were my precepts too present and too definite; they were also too universal to serve me in any given circumstance. Long years must pass before the truths we have made for ourselves become our very flesh.

Thus, instead of finding that I possessed the conditions of authorship, and those obstacles comparable to exterior forces which permit one to advance against one's first impulse, I was halted by ill-placed barriers, and I deliberately rendered things more difficult than they should have seemed to such young eyes. Meanwhile, in the other camp, I could see nothing but possibilities, whims, and disgusting facility: an effortless wealth, vain as that of dreams, moving and mingling the infinity of worn-out things.

If I began to write, and let chance direct my pen, I could only form words that bore witness to the impotence of the mind: *genius, mystery, profound* . . . attributes which properly belong to chaos, and tell less about their subject than about the writer. I tried to deceive myself, but this mental strategy was without success; I was so quick to answer my budding ideas with my pitiless maxims that the result of these transactions, at any given moment, was zero.

As a crowning misfortune, I worshipped precision; confusedly, it is true, but with passion; I vaguely laid claim to the right of directing my thoughts.

I felt, indeed, that the mind is forced to depend

189

on its own happy accidents; it is made for, creates, and receives the unforeseen; its definite hopes or efforts have no direct effects; and its decisions are useful only long afterwards—as if in a second life which the mind grants to the clearest part of itself. However, I did not believe in the innate power of delirium, in the necessity of ignorance, in flashes of absurdity, or in creative incoherence. What we derive from chance always resembles its parent.

Our revelations, so I reflected, are only events of a certain order; and we have still to interpret—we must always interpret—these *conscious events*. Even our happiest intuitions are in some sort inexact: *by excess,* as compared with our ordinary intelligence; *by deficiency,* as compared with the infinite complexity of the minute objects and real cases which they claim to bring under our sway. Our personal merit—after which we strive—consists not so much in feeling these inspirations as in seizing them, and not so much in seizing as in examining them. . . . And our riposte to our "genius" is sometimes worth more than its attack.

And besides, we know too well that chance is against this demon: the spirit whispers a million

shameless stupidities for every fine idea it abandons
to our grasp; and the value even of this millionth
chance depends on our ability to shape it to our
ends.—It is so with minerals, which have no value
in their veins and beds; they take on importance
only when brought to the light, and only through
the labour of refining.

Far from its being the intuitive elements which
give importance to works of art, subtract the
works, and your inspired lightnings will be no
more than intellectual accidents, lost in the statistics of the local life of the brain. The true value
of such inspirations does not depend on the ob-
scurity of their origin, or on the supposed depth
from which we are simple enough to believe that
they came, or on the exquisite surprise they cause to
ourselves; it depends rather on their meeting our
needs, and, in the final analysis, on the conscious
use we make of them—in other words, on the
collaboration of the whole man.

Once it is agreed that our greatest brilliance is
closely allied to our greatest chances of error,
and that the average of our thoughts is in some
sort insignificant—then it becomes evident that
our faculty of choosing and organizing is the part

of us which must ceaselessly be exerted. The rest,
which depends on nobody, is as useless to invoke
as the rain. One may baptize, deify, torment it
vainly; the only result will be the growth of simu-
lation and fraud—things so naturally attached to
the ambition of the mind that one hardly knows
whether they are its principle or its effect. The
disease of mistaking a hypallage for a discovery, a
metaphor for a demonstration, a vomit of words
for a torrent of important knowledge, and oneself
for an oracle—this curse is ours from birth.

Leonardo da Vinci has no connexion with these
disorders. Among the multitude of idols from
which we have to choose, since one of them at
least must be adored, he fixed his eyes on that
Obstinate Rigour which proclaims itself the most
exacting of them all. (And certainly it must be
the least vulgar, since all the others agree in hating
it.)

Once rigour has been instituted, a positive liberty is possible. Apparent liberty, on the other
hand, is only the privilege of obeying every chance
impulse; the more of it we possess, the more closely
we are chained to the same point; we are like a

cork on the sea, which is attached to nothing, which is attracted by everything, and over which all the forces of the universe contest and are cancelled off.

All the productions of the great Vinci can be deduced solely from his great purpose; and his thought, as if it belonged to no particular person, appears more universal, more detailed, more consecutive, and more isolated than the thought of any individual mind. The superior man is never an eccentric. His personality is as insignificant as you please. Few inequalities; no superstition of the intellect. No vain fears. He is not afraid of analysis; he guides it, or perhaps is guided by it, to remote consequences; he returns to the real without effort. He imitates; he innovates; he rejects neither the old because it is old, nor the new for being new; but he consults something in himself which is eternally of the present.

He was totally unaware of the coarsely defined opposition between the spirit of art and that of geometry which would be proclaimed, a century and a half later, by a man [1] who was entirely insensible to the arts, and could not conceive of this delicate, but natural, union of distinct gifts; who

[1] Pascal. *Tr.*

thought that painting is vanity and true eloquence
laughs eloquence to scorn; who involved us in a
wager where he lost all art and all geometry; who
finally, having changed his new lamps for old,
spent his time sewing papers in his pockets, when
it was the moment to give France the glory of
infinitesimal calculus. . . .

No revelations for Leonardo. No abyss that
opened by his side. An abyss would make him
think of a bridge. An abyss would serve for the
trial flights of some great mechanical bird.

And himself he might have considered as an
ideal thinking-animal, supple and responsive, endowed with several types of movement, capable
of passing from one gait to another at the rider's
slightest whim. The spirit of art, the spirit of geometry, he unites them both, abandons both, like
the successive paces of a well-trained horse. . . .
The supremely co-ordinated being has only to
make certain hidden and very simple modifications
of the will, and immediately he passes from the
category of purely formal transformations and
symbolic acts to that of imperfect knowledge and
spontaneous realities. To possess this liberty of
profound changes, to employ such a wide register

of adaptations, is merely to be a man in all his integrity, such a man as we imagine to have existed among the Greeks.

We are disconcerted by such superior elegance. This absence of embarrassment, of propheticism and patheticism; these precise ideals; this just balance between curiosity and ability, always restored by a master of equilibrium; this disdain for artifice and illusion; and, when displayed by the most ingenious of men, this ignorance of everything theatrical—such qualities, in our eyes, are so many scandals. For creatures like ourselves, who make a boast of our "sensibilities," think to possess everything in a few elementary effects of contrast and nervous resonance, and to apprehend everything when we give ourselves the illusion of being melted into the moving and iridescent substance of our life, what could be more difficult to conceive?

But Leonardo, very simply, as he passes from research to research, gains an ever more perfect mastery over his nature; he trains his thoughts with endless care, exercises his faculty of sight, develops his acts; he guides one hand or the other through admirably precise drawings; he expands and concentrates, tightens the relation between his desires and abilities, carries his reason into the realm of art, and preserves his grace.

An intelligence which has reached this degree of detachment will sometimes assume strange attitudes—like a dancer who surprises us by her ability to make, and for a time preserve, gestures of pure instability. The independence of Leonardo shocks our instincts and makes sport of our desires. There is nothing more free, that is to say, nothing less human, than his judgments on love and death. He lets them be inferred from a few fragments in his notebooks.

"Love in its fury"—he says in almost these words—"is such an ugly thing that the human race would die out (*la natura si perderebbe*) if those who practise it could see themselves." Many of his sketches are evidence of this scorn, for in certain matters the height of scorn is finally to examine them at leisure. Here and there he has drawn anatomical unions, horrible cross-sections of love itself. He is fascinated by the erotic machine, the mechanics of living bodies being his favourite domain; but the sweat of battle, the panting of the *opranti,* the monster formed of clashing muscular structures, and the final transfiguration into beasts—all this seems to excite only his repugnance and disdain.

His judgment on death must be reconstructed from a very short text, truly classical in its richness and simplicity. Perhaps it was meant to be placed in the introduction to a never-completed Treatise on the Human Body.

This man, who dissected ten cadavers to follow the course of a few veins, thinks to himself: The organization of our body is such a marvel of beauty that the soul, although *something divine,* is deeply grieved at being separated from the body which was its home.—*And I am sure,* says Leonardo, *that its tears and its sufferings are not unjustified.*

I will not discuss the kind of doubt, heavy with meaning, which these words imply. It is enough to consider the enormous shadow projected here by an idea in process of formation: death interpreted as a disaster *for the soul!* the death of the body as a diminution of this *divine thing!* Death moving the soul to tears and destroying its dearest work,

197

by the ruin of that structure which the soul had made for its dwelling!

I do not intend to deduce a Vincian metaphysic from these reticent words. However, I will permit myself a rather natural comparison, one which suggests itself to my mind. For such a student of organisms, the body is not something wholly contemptible, a mere rag; it has too many properties and resolves too many problems; *it possesses too many functions and resources not to answer some transcendent need, which is powerful enough to construct the body and not powerful enough to dispense with its complexity.* The body is the creation and the instrument of some one who has need of it, does not willingly cast it aside, and laments its loss as one might weep for vanished power. . . . Such is the feeling of Vinci. His philosophy is wholly *naturalistic*, outraged by *spiritualism*, firmly attached to the letter of the physico-mechanical explanation; however, on the subject of the soul, he is very close to the philosophy of Catholicism.

The Church, at least in so far as it is Thomist, does not grant a very enviable existence to the departed soul. There is nothing more destitute than this soul which has lost its body. It has scarcely more than being; it is a logical minimum, possessing a sort of latent life in which the soul is inconceivable to us, and doubtless to itself. Power, desire, and perhaps knowledge have been taken away. I am not even sure the soul can remember that somewhere, at some time, it was the *form* and *act* of its body. It is reduced to the honour of its autonomy. . . . Fortunately this vain and colourless condition is only temporary—if the word has any meaning outside the bounds of time. Reason demands, and dogma imposes, the restitution of the flesh.

The qualities of this supreme flesh will doubtless be far superior to those of the former body. Here it is necessary, I suppose, to conceive of something entirely different from a mere denial of Carnot's principle and a realization of the *improbable*. But it is useless to venture beyond the limits of physics, and to dream of a glorious body whose mass would be in a different relation than ours to universal gravity, while the ratio between this variable mass and the speed of light would be such that the promised *agility* could be attained. . . . In any case the departed soul must, according to theology, recover a certain functional life in a certain body, and, by means of this new body, a sort of matter which will allow it to function, and replenish its empty intellectual categories with incorruptible marvels.

A doctrine which concedes this almost primary importance to the bodily organism, and greatly reduces the function of the soul; which forbids and spares us the vain task of imagining the life of the soul after death; and which even goes so far as to oblige it to be reincarnated in order to participate in the full splendour of the eternal life—this doctrine, so exactly contrary to pure spiritualism, separates the Church in a most obvious manner from the majority of Christian sects.—But it would seem that during the last two or three centuries, religious literature has passed over no article more lightly. Apologists and preachers hardly speak of it. . . . The cause of this half-silence I do not know.

I have wandered so deeply into Leonardo that I do not know how to return directly to myself. . . . No matter: any path will lead me there; such is the definition of the self. It can never be lost; it can only lose its time.

So let us go a little farther down the slope, following the temptation of the mind. We can follow it without fear, unfortunately, for it leads to no real depth. Even our most "profound" thought is limited by the insuperable conditions which make all thought "superficial." We can penetrate only into a forest of transpositions; or rather, into a palace walled with mirrors, where a solitary lamp is multiplied to infinity.

But once more, let us see whether our curiosity, unaided, will bring to light the hidden system of an individual of the first magnitude; and let us imagine, as nearly as possible, how he must seem to his own eyes when sometimes he pauses in the course of his work to consider himself as a whole.

First he thinks of himself as subjected to common necessities and realities; and afterwards in relation to his secret of individual knowledge. He has our sort of vision, and a vision of his own. He has an opinion of his nature and a feeling of his artifice. He is absent and present. He maintains the sort of duality which priests must live. He knows that he cannot define himself entirely in terms of ordinary circumstances and motives. *To live,* and even to live well, is only a means for him; when he eats, he also nourishes a marvel which is not his life, and half his bread is consecrated. *To act* is still only an exercise. *To love* . . . but I doubt whether he finds it possible. As for glory, no. To shine in other eyes is only to see the glitter of false gems.

However, he must find some definite points of reference, and these must be so placed that he can use them to bring his particular life into harmony with the *generalized life* which he has discovered. The steady clairvoyance which seems (but without entirely convincing him) to represent the whole of himself, attempts to escape from the relativity it cannot fail to infer of everything else. But this apparent identity with the world, though it transforms itself, and is reproduced from day to day as pure as the sun, still carries within it the feeling of being a deception. It knows, in its fixity, that it is subjected to a mysterious force and an unseen modification; and hence is conscious that it always envelopes, even in its highest state of lucidity, a hidden possibility of failure and total ruin— just as the most coherent dream will contain an inexplicable germ of non-reality.

It is a sort of luminous torture to feel that one sees all, without ceasing to feel that one is still *visible*, and conceivably the object of hostile attention; and without ever finding that place and that vision which leave nothing behind them.

"*Durus est hic sermo*," the reader is about to say. But in these matters, whatever is not vague is difficult, and whatever is not difficult is nil. Let us go a little further.

For a presence of mind so thoroughly conscious of itself—which returns to itself by the detour of the "Universe"—all events and all categories of events—life, death, ideas—are only subordinate *symbols*. And since every *visible thing* is at the same time alien, indispensable, and inferior to the *thing that sees*, it results that the importance of these symbols, however great it may seem from moment to moment, tends on reflection to give way before the mere persistence of the attention we devote to them. Everything yields before the pure universality, the insurmountable generality, which consciousness feels itself to be.

If such events have the power of destroying the consciousness, they are, by the same token, robbed of all meaning; if they preserve it, they become part of its system. The intelligence is ignorant of its birth and does not know that it will perish. It is doubtless informed of its fluctuations and final obliteration, but only by means of an idea essentially no different from the others; and the mind might easily believe itself to be inalterable and eternal, had it not been led by its experiences, one day or another, to see various possibilities of ruin and the existence of a tendency which leads to the nethermost depths. This tendency, one feels, can become irresistible; it announces the beginning of a permanent separation from the spiritual sun; from the admirable maximum of clearness and solidity; from the greatest power of distinguishing and choosing. One has the impression of following this downward path, where it lies hidden by a thousand psychological impurities, and haunted by echoes and vertigo; it winds onward through the confusion of times and the disturbance of the functions; till finally, amidst an inexpressible disorder of the *dimensions* of knowledge, it leaves one stumbling toward that instantaneous and undivided state which snuffs this chaos into nothingness.

Nevertheless, a complete system of psychological substitutions is opposed to death, just as it is to life. As it grows more conscious and self-sufficient, it also becomes more completely detached from any origin, and, in some sort, less exposed to any chance of rupture. Like a ring of smoke, this system of interior energies miraculously lays claim to perfect independence and perfect indivisibility. Moreover, in a very clear consciousness, memory and events are so conjoined, expected, and meet with such quick response; the past is so well employed, the new so promptly balanced, and the relationship of the whole so clearly defined, that nothing, it seems, can begin and nothing end amid this almost pure activity. Apparently, by virtue of the perpetual exchange of *things* which constitutes this activity, it is assured of indefinite preservation, for it depends on no single one of these. It contains no *ultimate*—no particular object of thought or perception which is so much more real than all others that no other object can come after it. There is no idea which so completely fulfils the unknown conditions of the consciousness that it makes the consciousness disappear. No thought is such that it destroys, and concludes, the power of thinking—there is no given position of the bolt which closes the lock forever. And there is no particular thought whose relation to thought in general is that of a conclusion inherent in its development—resolving, like a final harmony, this permanent dissonance.

Since the mind has found no limits, and since no idea completes the task of the consciousness, it must perish in an incomprehensible event, predicted and prepared by those pangs and extraordinary sensations of which I spoke. These give a glimpse of unstable worlds, incompatible with the fulness of life; inhuman worlds, infirm worlds, comparable with those which the geometrician outlines by playing on axioms, and the physicist by supposing other than the admitted *constants*. Dreams, anxieties, and ecstasies; all those half-impossible states which might be described as introducing approximate values and irrational or transcendent solutions into the equation of knowledge, exist between the clearness of life and the simplicity of death, forming strange degrees, varieties, and ineffable phases—for there are no names for things among which one is quite alone.

Just as deceitful music unites the freedom of dreams with a consecutive logic born of extreme attention, and forms a synthesis of momentary moods, so the fluctuations of psychic equilibrium give a hint of the aberrant modes of existence.

Besides the ordinary forms of sensibility, we carry the germ of others which cannot thrive, but may be born. They are moments snatched from the implacable criticism of time. They cannot survive the complete functioning of our being: either we perish, or else they are dissolved. But they are monsters full of lessons, these monsters of the brain, these transitory conditions—spaces in which the known laws of continuity, connexion, and movement are altered; empires where light is associated with pain; electro-magnetic fields in which we follow strange circuits between the poles of fear and desire; matter composed of time; abysses literally of horror, love, or quietude; regions bizarrely welded to themselves, non-Archimedian realms which defy movement; sites perpetual in a lightning; hollow surfaces which are conjugated to our own nausea and inflected by our slightest intentions. . . . We cannot say they are real, and neither can we deny their reality. The man who has not traversed these states does not know the value of natural light or the most commonplace surroundings; he does not realize the true fragility of the world, which does not depend on the alternative of being or non-being; that would be too simple!—The wonder is not that things are, but

rather that they are such as they are, and not of a
different nature.   The *figure of this world* is one
of a family of figures, an infinite group of which
we possess all the elements, but without our knowledge.   This is the secret of inventors.

As it emerges from those intervals and personal
vagaries, into which not only physical weakness
and the presence of poisons in the nervous system,
but also the forces and subtleties of the attention,
the most exquisite logic, and a well-cultivated mysticism have diversely led the consciousness—the
latter comes to suspect that all accustomed reality
is only one solution, among many others, of universal problems.   It is convinced that things could
be *rather* different from what they are, without itself being *very* different from its present nature.
It dares to consider its "body" and its "world" as
almost arbitrary restrictions imposed on the extent
of its functions.   It thinks of itself as corresponding or replying, not to a *world*, but to some system
of a higher order, the elements of which are worlds.
It is able to form a greater number of mental combinations than its mode of life requires; it can act
with more rigour than any practical occasion de-

mands or tolerates; it deems itself more profound than the very abyss of bodily life and death; and this attention to its external circumstances cannot react upon itself, so far has it drawn aside from all things; so great are the pains it has taken *never to be a part of anything it might conceive or do.* It is reduced to a black mass which absorbs all light and gives nothing back.

Deriving a perilous courage from these exact remarks and inevitable pretensions; strong by virtue of the independence and changelessness it knows itself to possess, finally it claims to be the direct heir and living likeness of that being without form or beginning from whom derive, on whom devolve, all efforts to understand the cosmos. . . . A little more, and the consciousness will admit the necessary existence of only two entities, both essentially unknown: itself and x. Both abstractions, separate from all, implied by all, implying all. Equal and consubstantial.

The man who is led by the demands of the indefatigable mind to this contact with living shadows and this extreme of pure presence, perceives himself as destitute and bare, reduced to the su-

preme poverty of being a force without an object;
victim, masterpiece, accomplishment of simplifi-
cation and dialectics. His state is comparable with
that which is attained by the richest thought when
it becomes assimilated to itself, and recognized,
and consummated in a little group of characters
and symbols. The labour which we devote to an
object of reflection, he has expended on the subject
which reflects.

He exists without instincts, almost without
images; and he no longer has an aim. He resembles
nothing. I say *man*, and I say *he*, by analogy and
through lack of words.

The question is no longer one of choosing or
creating; of preserving oneself or expanding one's
capacities. There is nothing to be surmounted,
and there is not even the possibility of destroying
oneself.

All "genius" is now consumed; can no longer be
of any use. It was only a means of attaining the
final simplicity. There is no act of genius which
is not *less* than the act of being. A magnificent
law creates and informs the imbecile; the keenest
mind finds nothing better in itself.

Finally, being constrained to define itself by the sum total of things, and as being the *excess* of knowledge over this Whole, the perfected consciousness—which, to affirm itself, was forced to begin by denying an infinite number of elements an infinite number of times, and by exhausting the objects of its power without exhausting that power itself—now differs from nothingness by the smallest possible margin.

It makes one think naïvely of an invisible audience seated in the darkness of a theatre—a presence which cannot observe itself, is condemned to the adverse spectacle, and feels, nevertheless, that it composes all this breathless night. A complete, impenetrable, and absolute night; but swarming, eager, secretly organized, and composed of organisms that crowd and limit one another; a compact night, its shadows crammed with living organs which beat, respire, grow warm, and each of which, according to its nature, defends its place and function. Facing this intense and mysterious assemblage, and framed by a proscenium arch, all the Sensible, the Intelligible, and the Possible are seen to move and glitter. Nothing can be born or perish, exist in some degree, possess a time, a place, a form, a meaning—except on this definite *stage,* which the fates have circumscribed, and which, having separated it from I do not know what primordial confusion, as light was separated from darkness on the first day, they have opposed and subordinated to the condition of *being seen.*

If I have led you into this solitude, and even to this state of desperate clarity, it is only because the idea I formed of an intellectual power had to be carried to its final consequence. The characteristic of man is consciousness; and that of consciousness is a perpetual emptying, a process of detachment without cease or exception from anything presented to it, whatever that thing may be. An inexhaustible act, independent of the quality as of the quantity of things which appear; an act by which the *intellectual man* must finally reduce himself, deliberately, to an indefinite refusal to be anything whatsoever.

From this it results that all phenomena are struck with a sort of equal repulsion. Being rejected successively, as it were, by an identical gesture, they appear in a certain equivalence. Even one's

thoughts and feelings are enveloped in this uniform
condemnation, which extends to all perceptible
things. Nothing, it must be understood, escapes
this rigorous process of exhaustion; our mere attention to them suffices to put our inmost feelings
on a plane with exterior objects and events; the
moment they are observable, they go to join the
number of observed things.—Colour and sorrow;
memories, expectation, and surprise; this tree, and
the fluttering of its leaves, and its annual variation,
and its shadow like its substance, its accidents of
form or position, the far-away images which it
recalls to my idle mind—*all these things are equal.*
. . . Any one thing can be substituted for another—*may this not be the definition of things?*

It is inevitable that the mind should be led by its
own activity to this extreme and elementary act
of consideration. Its multiplied movements, its
inner struggles, perturbations, analytic returns—
do these leave anything unchanged? If so, what
is this changeless element? What is it that resists
the fascination of the senses, the dissipation of
ideas, the fading of memories, the slow variation
of the organism, the incessant and multiform ac-

tivity of the universe?—It is consciousness alone; the consciousness in its most abstract state.

Even our *personality*, which we thoughtlessly mistake for our deepest, our inmost characteristic and our sovereign good, is only a *thing*, both changeable and accidental, in comparison with the naked ego, the *I;* since we can think of our personality, calculate its interests, and even sometimes forget them. It is only a psychological deity of the second rank, which lives in our mirror and answers to our name. It belongs to the order of the Penates. It is subject to pain, greedy for incense like false gods, and like them is the temptation of worms. It blossoms under praise. It does not resist the power of wines, the delicacy of words, the sorcery of music. It is full of self-love, and for this reason is docile and easy to lead. It is dispersed in the carnival of madness, and yields bizarrely under the anamorphoses of dream. And still more: it is forced, painfully, to acknowledge the existence of equals, to confess that it is *inferior* to certain others; and this is a bitter recognition, an inexplicable fact.

Moreover, the personality is led in every way to admit that it is a mere phenomenon; that it must figure, along with all the accidents of the world, in tables and statistics; that its origin was a seminal chance and a miscroscopic incident; that it has run billions of risks, has been shaped by a quantity of coincidences, and is, in sum, however free or admirable, however definite or brilliant it may be, the result of an incalculable disorder.

Each person being a "sport of nature," *jeu de l'amour et du hasard,* it results that the highest ambition and even the deepest thoughts of this improvised creature are inevitably affected by their origin. His activity is always relative, and his masterpieces are casual. He thinks perishably, he thinks as an individual, he thinks by lucky flukes; and he merely blunders on the best of his ideas, since they spring from secret and fortuitous occasions which he hesitates to confess.—Besides, he is not even sure of being positively *some one;* he disguises and denies his nature more easily than he affirms it. Deriving a few resources and a great deal of vanity from his own inconsistency, he places his favourite activity in fictions. He lives on novels, seriously assumes a thousand rôles. His hero is never himself. . . .

And finally, he passes nine-tenths of his duration

215

in that which is not yet, in that which is no longer, in that which cannot be; to such an extent that our true *present* has nine chances in ten of never existing at all.

However, each individual possesses, at the depth where treasures are always buried, the fundamental permanence of a consciousness which depends on nothing. Just as the ear loses and rediscovers a grave and continuous sound which has never ceased to echo through the vicissitudes of a symphony, but has ceased from moment to moment to be heard—so the pure ego, the *I,* unique and monotonous element of each being, lost and rediscovered by itself, inhabits our senses eternally, and this profound *tone* of our existence, as soon as it is heard, dominates all the complicated conditions and varieties of existence.

To isolate this substantial attention from the strife of ordinary verities—is this not the ultimate and hidden task of the man with the greatest mind? And must he not come to define himself, as against all things, purely in terms of this unchangeable relationship between any and all objects—a definition which endows him with an almost inconceivable universality, and carries him, as it were, to the same power as the corresponding universe?—It is not his dear *person* which he raises to this high degree, since he has renounced his personality by making it the object of his thought, and has given the place of *subject* to that unqualifiable *I*, which has no name and history, which is neither more tangible nor less real than the center of gravity of a ring or of a planetary system—but which results from the whole, whatever that whole may be. . . .

A short while ago, the ostensible aim of this marvellous intellectual life was still . . . to wonder at itself. It was engrossed in the process of bringing forth offspring to admire; it confined itself to whatever was fairest, sweetest, brightest, and most solid; it was troubled only by being compared with the other mental organisms which were its rivals, being puzzled by the strangest problem one could possibly propound—which is actually propounded by the existence of others in our likeness; it consists, simply, in the possibility of other intelligences, in the plurality of the singular, in the contradictory co-existence of mutually independent durations—*tot capita, tot tempora,* as

many heads, so many times—a problem comparable with that of *relativity* in physics, but incom-
parably more difficult.

And now, carried away by his ambition to be
unique, guided by his ardour for omnipotence, the
man of great mind has gone beyond all creations,
all works, and even his own lofty designs; while at
the same time he has abandoned all tenderness for
himself and all preference for his own desires. In
an instant he immolates his individuality. He feels
that he is pure consciousness; two of these cannot
exist. He is the *I*, the universal pronoun, the ap-
pellation of *this* which has no connexion with a
body. Oh, to what point is his pride transformed,
and to what unplanned and unexpected goal has
he arrived! What moderation is the recompense
of all his triumphs! A life so firmly directed,
which has treated all the objects it might propose
to itself as obstacles, either to be avoided or overturned, was finally destined to an inexpugnable
conclusion, not a conclusion of its duration, but a
conclusion in itself. . . . To this point its pride
has led the mind, and here pride is consumed.
This directing pride abandons it, astonished, bare,
infinitely simple, on the pole of its treasures.

These thoughts are not mysterious. I might have written, more abstractly, that the most generalized group of our transformations, including all sensation, all ideas, all judgments, everything which is manifested *intus et extra*, admits an *invariable*.

I have allowed myself to exceed all the limits of patience and clarity, and have succumbed to the ideas which occurred to me while I was speaking of my task. In a few words I shall finish this somewhat simplified description of my state of mind; there are still some moments to pass in 1894.

Nothing is so curious as lucidity struggling with inadequacy. Approximately what happened, was destined to happen, and happened to me is this:

I was placed in the position of having to invent a character capable of a great number of accomplishments. I had one interest which was almost a mania: that is, I loved only the functioning of beings, and in works only their genesis. I knew that these works are always arrangements and falsifications, the *author* fortunately never being the *man*. The life of one is not the life of the other; accumulate all possible details on the life of Racine, and they will never teach you the art of writing verse. All criticism is dominated by the outworn principle that the man is the *cause* of his work—just as a criminal, in the eyes of the law, is the *cause* of the crime. They are far rather the effect! But this pragmatic principle lightens the task of the judge and the critic. Biography is easier than analysis, but on the questions which interest us most, it gives absolutely no information. . . . And more! The true life of a man, which is always ill-defined, even for his neighbours, even for himself, cannot be utilized in an explanation of his works, except indirectly and by means of a very careful elaboration.

Therefore no mistresses, no creditors; neither anecdotes nor adventures. We are guided instead to a more honest method: to imagine, excluding all these exterior details, a theoretical being, a psychological *model* more or less approximate, but representing in some sort our own capacity for reconstructing the work which we have set ourselves the task of explaining. Our success is very uncertain, but our labour is not vain; if it does not

resolve the insoluble problems of intellectual par-
thenogenesis, at least it states them with incomparable clearness.

Under the circumstances, this conviction was
my one positive resource.

The position in which I was placed, the total
elimination of all solutions antipathetic to my nature, the rejection of erudition and disdain for the
resources of rhetoric, all these left me in a state of
despair. . . . And in the end, I confess, my only
solution was to attribute my own agitation to the
unfortunate Leonardo, transporting the disorder
of my mind into the complexity of his. All my
desires I inflicted on him, as being things he possessed. I lent him many difficulties which were
haunting me in those days, as if he had met and
surmounted them. I changed my inadequacy
into his supposed power. I dared to consider myself under his name, and to utilize his person.

All this was false, but living. Consider a young
man of our time whose curiosity extends to a thousand things: may he not, after all, bear a rather
close resemblance to a man of the Renaissance?
He is naïve, but even his naïvety might serve to

represent that sort of relative naïvety *created* by four centuries of discoveries, to the detriment of the men who lived in that age. And besides, so I reflected, Hercules had no more muscles than we; they were merely larger. I cannot even budge the rock which he carried away, but the structure of our machines is no different; I correspond to him bone by bone, fibre by fibre, act by act, and our similarity allows me to imagine his labours.

A brief reflection on the matter leads to the conclusion that there is no other course to follow. The writer must put himself deliberately in the place of the being who occupies his thoughts. . . . And except for himself, who could answer when he evokes a mind? A mind is only to be found within oneself. It is our own functioning which, *alone*, can teach us something about any possible thing. Our knowledge, in my opinion, is limited only by the consciousness we can possibly have of our being—and perhaps of *our bodies*. Whatever x may be, the idea which I form of it, if carried toward the extreme, tends toward myself, whatever I may be. One may recognize this truth or fail to comprehend; one may either submit to or desire it, but there is no escape, no other issue. It

is with our own substance that we imagine and
form a stone, a plant, a movement, an *object;*
any given image is no more, perhaps, than a beginning of ourselves. . . .

> *lionardo mio*
> *o lionardo che tanto penate . . .*

As for the true Leonardo, he was what he was.
. . . However, this myth, which is stranger than
all the others, gains infinitely by being moved from
fable into history. The further one proceeds, the
more precisely he grows. The experiments of Ader
and the Wrights have bathed his treatise *On the
Flight of Birds* in a sort of retrospective glory;
while the germ of Fresnel's theories is found in
certain passages of the manuscripts preserved at
the Institut de France. In the course of the last
few years, the researches of the regretted M. Du-
hem on the *Origins of Statics* have made it possible
to attribute to Leonardo the fundamental theorem
of the parallelogram of forces, and a very clear—
though incomplete—notion of the principle of vir-
tual work.

II

INTRODUCTION

(1894)

To Marcel Schwob

O F A man there remain the dreams which his name inspires, and the works which make that name a symbol of admiration, hate, or indifference. We think that he once thought, and can rediscover among his works a thought which really derives from us; this thought we can remake into the image of our own. It is easy to represent an ordinary man; our own simple memories restore his motives and elementary reactions. The indifferent acts which constitute the exterior of his life, and those which form the semblance of ourselves, are linked by the same causation. We can serve as the bond of these acts as well as he; and the circle of activity which his name suggests is no wider than ours. On the other hand, if we choose an individual who excels in some respect,

224

we shall find it more difficult to imagine the paths
and labours of his mind; and, in order not to be
restricted to a confused admiration, we shall be
forced to expand our conception of his dominating
quality, which we doubtless possess only in the
germ. However, if all the faculties of the chosen
mind are widely developed at the same time, or
if considerable traces of its activity are to be found
in all fields of endeavour, then the figure of our
hero grows more and more difficult to conceive in
its unity, and tends to escape our efforts. From
one extreme to the other of this mental territory,
there are such great distances which we have never
travelled. Our understanding fails to grasp the
continuity of this whole—just as it fails to perceive those formless rags of space which separate
known objects and are subject to the chance of
intervals; and just as it loses myriads of facts from
moment to moment, perceiving only the small
number which can be evoked by speech. However,
we must delay over the task, become inured to its
difficulties; and, if our imagination suffers from
its efforts to grasp this combination of apparently
heterogeneous elements, we must learn to with-
stand the pain.

In this process, all our intelligence is applied to conceiving a unique order and a single motive force. We desire to place a creature in our likeness at the heart of the system we impose on ourselves. We struggle to form a decisive image. And our mind, with a violence proportionate to its lucidity and breadth, ends by reconquering its own unity. As if by the action of a machine, an hypothesis takes shape; it proves to be the individual who performed all these deeds, the central vision where all must have taken place, the monstrous brain or strange animal which wove thousands of pure bonds between so many forms. Those enigmatic and diverse constructions were the labours of this brain, its instinct making an abode. . . . The production of such an hypothesis is a phenomenon which admits of variations, but not of chance. Its value is the same as that of the logical analysis whose object it should be. And it is the basis of the method which will occupy and serve us.

I propose to imagine a man who shall have performed actions so thoroughly distinct that, if I succeed in postulating the general purpose which lies behind them, none could be more universal. And I should like this man to possess an infinitely keen perception of the difference of things, the adventures of which perception might well be called analysis. All the world is his objective and his guide; he thinks of the universe continually, and of rigour.[1] He is so formed as to forget nothing which enters into the confusion of things; not the least shrub. He descends into the depths of that which exists for all men; he wanders apart and examines himself. He learns to know the habits and structures of nature, works on them from every angle, and finally it is he alone who constructs, enumerates, sets in motion. He builds churches and fortresses; he fashions ornaments full of harmony and grandeur; he makes a thousand curious engines, and performs the rigorous calculations of many a research. He abandons the debris of nobody knows what grandiose games. In the midst of these pastimes, which are mingled with his science, which in turn cannot be distinguished from a passion, he has the charm of always seeming to think of something else. . . . I shall follow him as he moves through raw unity and the substance of the world, where he will become so familiar with nature that he will imitate in order to touch it, and

[1] *Hostinato rigore*, obstinate rigour—the motto of Leonardo.

227

will end in the difficulty of conceiving an object which it does not contain.

This creature of thought requires a name, to limit the expansion of terms too far removed from ordinary usage, too difficult to grasp. I can find none more suitable than that of *Leonardo da Vinci*. Whoever represents a tree must also represent the background from which the tree stands forth. The logic of this is almost tangible and almost unknown. The individual I am going to discuss can be reduced to a deduction of this nature. Very little of what I say should be understood of the man who rendered this name illustrious; I am not pursuing a coincidence which is impossible to define incorrectly. I am trying to give a detailed view of an intellectual life; one suggestion of the methods which every discovery implies, *one*, chosen among the multitude of imaginable things—a crude model, if you will, but preferable in every way to a string of doubtful anecdotes, a commentary from an art catalogue, or a list of dates. Such erudition would be false to the purely hypothetical intention of this essay. I am not a stranger to learning of this sort, but my task is not to mention it, so that a conjecture relating to very general terms may not be confused with the exterior fragments of a personality so thoroughly forgotten that they leave us convinced both of his thinking existence and of the impossibility of ever knowing it better.

Many an error which distorts our judgment of human achievements is due to a strange disregard of their genesis. Seldom does one remember that they did not always exist. From this arises a sort of reciprocal coquetry, which generally results in authors' failing to discuss, and even in their concealing, the origins of a work. We fear that they are humble; we even suspect them of being natural. And, although few authors have the courage to say how their work took shape, I believe that there are very few more who risk even a knowledge of this process. Such a research begins by one's abandoning all notions of glory and all laudatory epithets; it does not permit of any idea of superiority or delusion of grandeur. It leads to the discovery of the relativity which underlies the apparent perfection. And it is necessary, for only in this way can we avoid believing that minds differ as radically as their productions would make it seem.

Certain works of science, particularly those of mathematicians, flow so limpidly from conclusion to conclusion that one can hardly believe they have an author. There is something inhuman about them, and this quality has not been without its effect. It has led to the belief that great distances exist between certain studies: as, for example, between the arts and the sciences; with the result that the minds devoted to each have also been separated by the general opinion, and set as widely apart as the results of their labours seemed to be. These labours, however, differ only by variations from a common basis—by the part of that basis which each preserves, and the part which each neglects, in forming their languages and symbols. Hence, we must be a little suspicious of books and expositions which seem too pure, too free from alien elements. Whatever is fixed deceives us, and whatever is made with the idea of being seen is apt to assume an air of nobility. The operations of the mind can serve our purpose of analysis only while they are moving, unresolved, still at the mercy of a moment—before they have been given the name of laws, entertainments, theorems, or works of art, and, being perfected, have lost their mutual resemblance.

Within the mind, there is a drama. Drama, adventure, agitation, all words of this category can be employed on condition that several are used, and are corrected one by the other. Such dramas are generally lost, like the plays of Menander. However, we preserve the manuscripts of Leonardo and Pascal's illustrious notes. These fragments demand our attention. Having examined them, we can guess by what starts and snatches of thought, by what strange suggestions from human events or the flow of sensations, and after what immense moments of lassitude, men are able to see the shadows of their future works, the ghosts which precede. For examples of this process, we need not have recourse to great men, since it would be argued that they were exceptions; we need only observe some one who thinks himself alone and abandons himself to impulse; he *recoils* from an idea; *grasps* it; denies, smiles, or shrinks back, and mimics the strange condition of his own diversity. Madmen often act like this in public.

231

By such examples, physical movements which can be measured and defined are linked with the personal drama of which I was speaking. The actors in that drama are mental images. It is easy to understand that, by eliminating the individual peculiarities of these images, and considering only their succession, frequency, periodicity, varying facility of association, and finally their duration, one is quickly led to find analogies in the so-called material world. We compare them with scientific analyses; we postulate an environment, continuity, velocities, properties of displacement, and later, masses and energy. Thereupon we decide that many such systems are possible, that any one of them is worth no more than another, and that our use of them—always valuable, since it always explains something—must be continually supervised and restored to its purely verbal rôle. For analogy, in reality, is only the power of causing images to vary; of combining them, making part of one co-exist with part of another, and perceiving, voluntarily or involuntarily, the relation between their structures. This renders it impossible to describe the mind which is their scene. For here, words lose their virtue. Here they are formed; here they gush forth, under its *eyes*: it is the mind which describes words to us.

And so man sets out with visions, whose power makes his own. He comes back with his history, of which his visions are the geometrical bond. From this process arise those decisions which astonish us; those perspectives, miraculous divinations, exact judgments, illuminations, and incomprehensible anxieties; also many blunders. In certain extraordinary cases, while invoking abstract gods—genius, inspiration, a thousand others—one asks with amazement whence these marvels have come. And once again we believe that something has been created, for we worship mystery and the marvellous as much as we ignore their sources; we ascribe logic to miracle, although the inspired author had been ready for a year. He was ripe. Always he had thought of this work, perhaps without suspecting the fact; and while others were not yet in a state to see, he had examined, organized, and now was doing no more than to read what was written in his mind. The secret—that of Leonardo and that of Bonaparte, like that which the highest intelligence once possessed—resides and can only reside in the relations which they found—

which they were forced to find—*between things of which we cannot grasp the law of continuity.* It is certain that, on reaching the decisive moment, they had only to accomplish certain definite acts. Their supreme achievement, the one which the world admires, was only a simple matter, like comparing two lengths.

From this point of view, the unity of the method we are discussing is evident. Here, among the processes of creation, it is native and elementary. This method is their very life; their definition. And when beings as profound as the man of whom I am thinking in these pages, discover the secret resources of this method, they have the right to exclaim, in a clearer and more conscious moment: *"Facil cosa è farsi universale*—It is easy to make oneself universal!" They can, for a moment, admire the prodigious instrument which they are— at the price of instantly denying a miracle.

But this final clarity is attained only after long wanderings and indispensable idolatries. A consciousness of the operations of thought, which is the disregarded logic of which I spoke, is a power which exists but rarely, even in the keenest minds. The number of conceptions, the power to prolong them, and the abundance of discoveries are something quite separate, and are produced without reference to one's opinion of their nature. And yet the importance of this opinion is easy to realize. A flower, a proposition, a sound can be imagined almost simultaneously; the intervals between them can be made as short as you choose; and any one of these objects of thought can also change, be deformed, lose its initial qualities successively at the will of the mind which conceives it—but it is only in one's consciousness of this power that all its worth resides. This alone permits us to criticize these *formations*, to interpret them, to find in them nothing more than they contain, and not to confuse their states with that of reality.

With the attainment of this consciousness begins the analysis of all intellectual phases; of all the states which it can describe as fallacy, madness, discovery—which before were only nuances, not to be distinguished one from the other. They were equivalent variations of a common substance, which were comparable one to the other, existed at indefinite and almost irresponsible levels, could sometimes be named, and all belonged to the same category. To be conscious of one's thoughts, in so far as they are thoughts, is to recognize this sort of equality or homogeneity; to feel that all combinations of the sort are natural and legitimate, and that one's method should consist in stimulating them, in seeing them distinctly, in seeking to learn what they imply.

At a given point in this process of observation; this double intellectual life which makes ordinary thought seem nothing more than the dream of a waking sleeper, it appears that the progression of this dream—with its mass of combinations, contrasts and perceptions, grouped about a research or advancing indeterminately, as one desires—is developed with *perceptible* regularity; with the evident continuity of a machine. Thence arises the idea (or the wish) to hasten the course of this progression; to carry its terms to their *limit*, or to that of their imaginable expression, *after which everything will be changed*. And if this mode of being conscious becomes habitual, one will be led, for example, to examine beforehand all the possible results of an imagined act and all relationships of a conceived object. In this manner one acquires the faculty of putting them aside, of always divining something more exact or intense than the given object, and of rousing oneself from any thought which was lasting too long. A thought which becomes fixed, whatever its nature may be, assumes the characteristics of an hypnosis, and is called, in the language of logic, an idol; in the domain of art and poetic construction it becomes a fruitless monotony.

The method I am discussing is the condition of all generalization. It leads the mind to foresee its own actions, to imagine as a whole whatever was going to be imagined in detail, and to picture the effect of the succession thus briefly summarized. In certain individuals, this form of consciousness becomes a veritable passion, remarkable for its energy. In the arts, it is the cause of each separate advance, and explains the continually more frequent use of contracted terms, of suggestion, of violent contrasts. And this same method exists implicitly, in its rational form, at the basis of all mathematical concepts. It is very similar to the method which, under the name of reasoning by recurrence,[2] extends the application of these con-

---

[2] The philosophical importance of this form of reasoning was demonstrated for the first time by M. Poincaré in a recent article. When consulted by the author, the illustrious mathematician confirmed our statement of his priority.

cepts—and which, from the type of simple addition to infinitesimal summation, does more than to spare an indefinite number of useless experiments; it produces more complex ideas, since the imitation of my act is a new act, enveloping all possible adaptations of the first.

To this drama, picture, agitation, lucidity . . . we naturally oppose other scenes and movements, which we group together and call "Nature" or "the World." But we can do nothing with this external nature except to distinguish it from ourselves, and then immediately replace ourselves within its frame.

The philosophers have generally ended by implying our existence in the notion we hold of nature, and our notion of nature in that which we hold of ourselves; but they rarely go beyond this point, for we know that their aim is rather to criticize the ideas of their predecessors than to form new concepts of their own. Scientists and artists have employed the notion of nature in their different fashions; the first measured and then constructed; the second constructed as if they had measured already. Everything they have made takes its natural place in the external world, and there plays its part, changing this world by giving new forms to its elements. However, before classifying and building, we observe; there are a host of qualities which present themselves, and from this number our senses, each in its different way and with its different degree of docility, distinguish and choose those which will be retained by the individual. At first this process of recognition is undergone passively, almost unconsciously, as a vessel lets itself be filled; there is a feeling of slow and pleasurable circulation. Later one becomes interested, and gives other values to things which had seemed closed and irreducible; one adds to them, takes more pleasure in particular features, and finally expresses these—an act which is like transmitting or restoring an energy received through the senses. Soon this energy will alter the environment in its turn, employing to this end the conscious thought of a person.

The universal man also begins by merely contemplating, and always returns to the process of being impregnated with spectacles. He always comes back to the intoxication of the particular instinct and to the emotion derived from the least of real things, when one considers both thing and instinct—each so distinct in all its qualities, each of them concentrating, in every manner, so many effects.

The majority of people see with their intellect much more frequently than with their eyes. Instead of coloured spaces, they are aware of concepts. Something whitish, cubical, erect, its planes broken by the sparkle of glass, is immediately a house for them—the House! A complex idea, a combination of abstract qualities. If they walk forward, the surfaces will be altered, the windows will move in a file; but this they will fail to observe, for their concept remains unchanged. They perceive with a dictionary instead of with their retina; and they approach objects so blindly, they have such vague knowledge of the pains and pleasures of vision, that they have invented *beautiful views*. Of the rest, they are unaware. However, in this one instance, they feast on a concept rich in words.

(A general law of that weakness which exists in all domains of knowledge is precisely our choice of *obvious* standpoints, our being content with definite systems, which facilitate, make it easy to grasp. . . . Hence, one can say that a work of art is always more or less didactic.)

Even these beautiful views are more or less closed to ordinary observers. And all the modulations so delicately contrived by little movements, changing light, and tiring eyes are lost to them, neither adding to nor substracting from their sensations. Since they know that the level of still waters is horizontal, they fail to observe that the sea is *upright* at the horizon; and should the tip of a nose, the segment of a shoulder or two separate fingers happen to dip into a pool of light which isolates them, our observers never take the pains to regard them as a new jewel, enriching their vision. This jewel is a fragment of a person, and the person alone exists, is known to them. And, since they utterly reject everything which lacks a name, the number of their impressions is strictly limited in advance! [3]

[3] See Proposition CCLXXI of Leonardo's treatise *On Painting*: "Impossibile che una memoria possa riserbare tutti gli aspetti o mutazioni d'alcun membro di qualunque animal si sia. . . . È perche ogni quantita continua è divisibile in infinito. . . . It is impossible for any memory

The use of the opposite gift leads to analysis in the true sense of the word. One cannot say that it is exercised in *nature*. This word, although it seems general, and appears to contain every possibility of experience, is altogether personal. It evokes particular images, determined by the memory or history of one man. In most cases it calls forth the vision of a green, vague, and continuous eruption, of some great elementary work opposed to everything human, of a monotonous quantity which will some day cover us; finally of something stronger than we, which entangles and rends itself; which sleeps on, works on; and to which, personified, the poets accord bounty, cruelty, and several other intentions. . . . Hence, our imaginary observer must be placed not in nature, as we imagine it, but in it matters not what corner of existence.

to retain all the aspects of any member of any animal whatsoever. This is because any continuous quantity is infinitely divisible."

What I have said of sight also applies to the other senses, although I believe that sight is the most *intellectual* of them all. In the mind, visual images predominate. It is between these images that the faculty of analogy is most often exercised. When we make analogies between any two objects, the inferior term of this comparison may even originate in an error of judgment accompanying an indistinct sensation. . . . Moreover, the form and colour of an object are so evidently foremost that they enter into our concepts of qualities relating to another sense. If we speak, for example, of the hardness of iron, the visual image of iron will almost always be produced, and rarely an auditory image.

The observer is caged in a sphere which is never broken. It has variations which will later be movements or objects; and its surface remains closed, although every portion of the sphere is renewed and changes position. At first the observer is only the condition of this finite space; we might say that from moment to moment he *is* this finite space. He is troubled by none of his memories or powers so long as he is equal to what he sees. And if I were able to imagine his remaining in this state, I should say that his impressions hardly differed from those of a dream. He is vaguely conscious of pleasure, pain, and a sense of tranquillity,[4] all imparted to him by these indefinite forms, among which is numbered his own body. And now, slowly, some begin to be forgotten, almost disappearing from sight; while others succeed in being seen—without changing their place. It must also be remarked that changes in vision resulting from the mere duration of one's attention, and from tired eyes, are apt to be confused with those due to the movement of

---

[4] Without touching on physiological question, I might mention the case of a man suffering from depressant insanity. This patient, whom I saw once in a clinic, was in a state of retarded life; he recognized objects only after an extraordinary delay. Sensations took a very long time to reach his brain. He felt no needs. This form of insanity is exceedingly rare.

the objects observed. Certain areas in the extent of this vision are exaggerated, in the same way that an ailing member seems larger, and, because of the importance which it acquires from pain, distorts our idea of our body. These exaggerated areas will seem easier to remember, more pleasurable to observe. And it is from observing them that the spectator rises out of mere perception to reverie; henceforth he will be able to extend the particular characteristics derived from the first and most familiar objects to other objects in greater and greater number.

Remembering a precedent, he will perfect the given space. Then, at his pleasure, he will arrange and analyze his successive impressions. He is now able to appreciate the value of strange combinations. A group of men, a bunch of flowers, a hand, a cheek which he isolates, a spot of sunlight on a wall, a chance group of animals—all these he regards as complete and solid beings. From perceiving some of their parts, he feels the desire to form invisible wholes. Thus, he infers the planes outlined by a bird in its flight, the curve drawn by a pitched ball, the surfaces defined by our gestures, and the extraordinary gaps, the fluid arabesques, the formless chambers created in an all-penetrating network by the grating and tremulous flight of insects, by trees which roll like ships, by wheels, the human smile, the tide. Sometimes the traces of what he imagined can be seen on the waters or the sand; sometimes his own retina, in the course of time, can compare some object with the form of its movement.

There is a natural transition from such forms, which are born of movement, to those movements which become forms by the aid of a simple change in duration. If a drop of rain appears to be a line, a thousand vibrations to be a continuous sound, and the irregularities of this paper to be a polished plane; and if the duration of these impressions is their sole cause—then a stable form may be replaced by a sufficient rapidity in the periodic transfer of a well-chosen thing (or element). Mathematicians will be able to introduce time and velocity into the study of forms, just as they can eliminate both from the study of movements. In common speech, by a similar process, a road will *climb*, a jetty *stretch*, a statue *rise*. And, by dizzy analogies and the logic of continuity, these actions will be carried to the limit of their tendency, to the impossibility of their ever halting.

Everything moves to some extent, imaginarily. In this chamber, and because I concentrate on this one thought, the objects about me *act*; the flame of the lamp is not the only moving thing. The armchair rots away in its place, the table revolves so quickly that it is motionless, and the curtains flow endlessly, continuously. The result is an infinite complexity. Struggling to regain command of ourselves in the midst of these moving bodies, the circulation of their contours, the jumble of knots, the paths, the falls, the whirlpools, and the group of assorted velocities, we must have recourse to our great power, that of deliberately forgetting—and, without destroying the acquired idea, we introduce a generalized concept—that of the orders of magnitude.

And so expires, in the expansion of our data, our intoxication with particular objects—of which there can be no science. When observed for a long time, and if one thinks of them, they change; and if one does not think of them, one falls into a lasting torpor, of somewhat the same nature as a tranquil dream; one stares hypnotically at the corner of a table or the shadow of a leaf, only to waken as soon as they are *seen*.

Certain men feel with special delicacy the pleasure which derives from the *individuality* of objects. What they prefer in a thing, and what causes their delight, is the quality of being unique—which all things possess. Their form of curiosity finds its ultimate expression in fiction and the arts of the theatre; it is called, at this extreme, the *faculty of identification*.[5] Nothing seems more deliberately absurd when described than the temerity of a person who declares that he *is* a certain object and feels its impressions—especially if this object is material.[6] And yet there is nothing more powerful in the imaginative life. The chosen object becomes, as it were, the centre of this life—a centre of associations which are more or less numerous according to whether the object is more or less complex. Fundamentally this faculty must be a means of exciting the imaginative vitality, of setting potential energy to work. Carried too far, it becomes a pathological symptom, and gains a frightful ascendancy over the increasing feebleness of a decaying mind.

[5] Edgar Allan Poe, *On Shakespeare* (*Marginalia*).

[6] Whoever explains why the identification with a material object *seems* more absurd than that with a living object, will have made a step toward explaining the problem.

From the mere observation of things to these complex states, the mind has only enlarged its functions, forming concepts which reply to the problems offered by all sensation, and solving these problems more or less easily, according to whether a larger or smaller production of such concepts is demanded. It is evident that we are touching, at this point, on the *method proper* of thought. Thinking consists, during almost all the time which we devote to it, in wandering among leitmotifs about which we can only be certain that we know them more or less well. Hence, things can be classified according to the ease or difficulty they afford to our comprehension, according to our degree of familiarity with them, and according to the various resistances offered by their parts or conditions when we try to imagine them together. The history of this graduation of complexity remains to be conjectured.

The world is irregularly strewn with regular arrangements. Crystals are of this nature; so are flowers and leaves, many striped or spotted ornaments on the furs, wings, or shells of animals, the traces of wind on water or sand, etc. Sometimes these effects depend on a sort of perspective and on unstable groupings. Distance produces or deforms them. Time displays or veils them. Thus, the number of deaths, births, crimes, and accidents presents a regularity in its variation, which becomes more and more obvious as we follow its record through the years. The most surprising events, and the most *asymmetrical* in relation to their neighbouring moments, return to a semblance of order when considered in relation to longer periods. One might also cite the examples of instincts, habits, and customs, and even the appearances of periodicity which have given rise to so many systems of historical philosophy.

The study of regular combinations belongs to the different sciences and, when it can be assimilated to none of these, to the calculation of probabilities. For our purpose, we need only the observation made on introducing this topic: regular combinations, whether of time or space, are irregularly distributed in our field of investigation. Mentally, they seem to be opposed to a vast number of formless things.

They might well be described as "the first guides of the human mind," except that such a proposition would be immediately convertible into other terms. In any case, they represent continuity.[7] A thought permits of a change or transfer (of attention, for example) among elements which apparently are fixed in their relation to this thought, and which are selected by it from memory or immediate perceptions. If these elements are perfectly similar, or if their difference can be reduced to mere distance, to the elementary fact of their not being confused, then the labour to be performed is in turn reduced to this purely differential notion. Thus, a straight line will be the easiest of all lines to conceive, because there is no smaller effort for the mind than that exerted in passing from one point of a straight line to another, each of these points being similarly placed in regard to all the others. In other words, all portions of a straight line are so homogeneous, however short we may conceive them to be, that all of them can be reduced to one, always the same; and this is the reason why the dimensions of figures are always

[7] Here I do not employ this word in its mathematical sense. It is not a question of inserting a numerable infinity and an innumerable infinity of values into an interval; it is only a question of direct intuition, of objects which suggest laws, and of laws which are evident to the eyes. The existence or possibility of such laws is the first fact of this order, and not the least important.

reduced to straight lines. At a higher degree of complexity, periodicity is employed to represent continuous properties; for this periodicity, whether it exists in space or time, is nothing else than the division of an object of thought into fragments of such nature that they can be replaced one by the other—or else it is the multiplication of an object under the same conditions.

Why is it that only a part of existence can be so reduced? There is a moment when the figure becomes so complex, or the event appears so new, that we must renounce the attempt to consider one or the other as a whole, or to proceed with their translation into continuous values. At what point did our Euclids halt in their apprehension of forms? What was the particular degree of interruption which set a limit to their conception of continuity? Whatever this point may be, it is the furthest extreme of a research into which one cannot fail to be tempted by the doctrines of evolution. We hesitate to confess that this limit can be final.

It is certain, in any case, that the basis and aim of all speculations is the the extension of continuity by the aid of metaphors, abstractions, and modes of speech. These are employed by the arts in a fashion of which we shall speak hereafter.

We arrive at the conception that parts of the world can be reduced to intelligible elements. Sometimes our senses suffice; at other times the most ingenious methods must be employed; but always there are voids. The attempts remain imperfect. And here is the kingdom of our hero. He has an extraordinary sense of the symmetry which makes him regard everything as a problem. He introduces the creations of his mind into every fissure of the understanding. It is evident how extraordinarily convenient he can be. He is like a scientific hypothesis. We should have to invent him, but he exists; the universal man can now be imagined. We have reached the point where a Leonardo da Vinci can exist as a concept in our minds, without immeasurably dazzling them. Our dream of his power need not be too quickly lost in a fog of the great words and magnificent epithets which are so friendly to inconsistent thought. Do you believe that Leonardo himself would be satisfied with such mirages?

This *symbolic* mind preserved an immense col-

lection of forms, a treasure always rich with the attitudes of nature, a potentiality always ready to be
translated into action, and growing with the extension of its domain. A host of concepts, a host
of possible memories, the power to choose an extraordinary number of distinct things from the
world at large, and to arrange them in a million
ways—these elements composed the mind of
Leonardo. He was the master of faces, anatomies,
machines. He knew how a smile is made; he could
reproduce it on the façade of a house or in the
mazes of a garden. He ravelled, and he unravelled,
filaments of water and tongues of fire. If his hand
happened to trace the peripeties of the attacks
which he had planned, the trajectories of balls from
thousands of cannon were described in fearful
bouquets; they razed the bastions of cities and
strongholds which, only a moment past, he had
constructed in all their details, and fortified. As
if, when he observed them in a calm, he found the
metamorphoses of things too gradual, he adored
battles, tempests, the deluge. Regarding them
from a height, he could see them as a mechanical
process; and he could feel them in the apparent
independence or life of their fragments—for ex-

ample, in a handful of sand driven before the wind, or in the stray thought of each soldier, distorted by passion and inner torment.[8] The little bodies of children, "timid and brusque," were known to him, as were the limited gestures of women and old men, and the simplicity of the corpse. He had the secret of composing fantastic beings, and of making their existence seem probable; the logic which harmonizes their discordant parts is so rigorous that it suggests the life and naturalness of the whole. He made a Christ, an angel, a monster, by taking that which is known, which exists everywhere, and arranging it in a new order. Here he profits by the illusion of painting, an art which depicts only a single quality of things, and thereby evokes all their qualities.

He passed from the slow or headlong movement of the avalanche and from massive curves to multitudinous draperies; from smoke which blossoms on the roof to distant clumps of trees and the misty beeches of the horizon; from fish to birds; from the sea glittering in the sun to birch leaves in their thousand slender mirrors; from the scales of fish

[8] See the description of a battle, of the deluge, etc., in his treatise *On Painting*, and in the manuscripts at the Institut de France. Drawings of tempests, bombardments, etc., can be seen in the Windsor manuscripts.

to the march of lightning over gulfs; from ears
and curls to the frozen whirlpools of the nautilus.
From the shell he proceeded to the spiral tumour of
the waves, and from the surface of tidal pools to
the veins which carry the water in, thence passing to the elementary gestures of crawling and to
fluid serpents. He vivified. He moulded the water
around a swimmer [9] into clinging scarves, which
show the effort of the muscles in relief. As for
the air, it was fixed in the wake of soaring larks; he
pictured it in the shreds of shadow and the froth
of those escaping bubbles which such aerial trav-
ellers must disturb, and which they leave trailing
across the blue-tinted pages of space, through all
the vague crystal of space.

He reconstructed all buildings; he was tempted
by every mode of expression and every type of material. He possessed all things distributed in the
dimensions of space; he was master of vaults and
beams and soaring domes; of galleries and loggias
in ranks; of masses held in the air by arches; of
bridges flung from pier to pier; of trees deep in
verdure, marching into the atmosphere from which
they drink; and of the structures formed by mi-

[9] Sketch in the manuscripts of the Institut de France.

gratory birds—those acute triangles pointing to the South which show a rational combination of living beings.

He made sport of difficulties; and growing bolder, he translated all sentiments into the clarity of his universal language. The abundance of his metaphorical resources made these feats possible. His desire utterly to probe the slightest fragment, the least splinter of the world, renewed the force and cohesion of his being. His joy can be read in his decorations for fêtes and in other charming inventions; when he dreamed of constructing a *flying man,* he would have him rise to seek snow on the mountaintops and, returning, scatter it over the streets of cities which pulse with the heat of summer. His emotion delighted in pure faces touched by a pouting shadow, and in the gesture of a silent god. His hate employed all weapons: all the artifices of the engineer, all the stratagems of the general. He established terrible engines of war, and protected them with bastions, caponiers, salients, and with moats which he provided with water gates, so as suddenly to transform the aspect of a siege; and I remember—meanwhile enjoying this fine Italian wariness of the *cinquecento*—that he

built donjons in which four flights of stairs, independent round the same axis, separated the mercen-
aries from their leaders, and the troops of hired
soldiers one from the other.

He worshipped the human body, which measures and is measured by all things. He was aware
of its height—that a rose can come to its lips, and
a great plane-tree surpass it twenty times, while
dropping a spray of leaves to the height of a man's
head. He knew that a radiant body will fill a given
room, or the concavity of a vault which is deduced
from the human form, or a landscape which counts
the steps of man. He overheard the light fall of a
foot; and he spied on the skeleton silent in its
flesh, on the accidents of the human walk, on all
the superficial play of heat and coolness over
nudities—perceiving them as a diffused whiteness
or a sheet of bronze, welded to a mechanism. And
the face, that enlightening and enlightened thing;
of all visible things the most individual, the most
magnetic, the most difficult to regard without reading therein—the face would always haunt him. In
each man's memory, there are a few hundred faces
with their vague variations. In his, they were classified and proceeded consecutively from one physi-

ognomy to another, from one irony to another, from one wisdom to a lesser, from kindness to divinity—by symmetry. About the eyes—fixed points of variable brilliance—he adjusted the mask which hides a complex structure of bones and distinct muscles under a uniform skin; drawing the mask taut, he made it reveal all.

Among the multitude of minds, that of Leonardo impresses us as being one of those *regular combinations* which were mentioned above. Unlike most of the others, he need not be attached, in order to be understood, to a particular nation, a tradition, or a group exercising the same art. His acts, by virtue of their number and intercommunication, together form a symmetrical object—a sort of *system complete in itself,* or completing itself incessantly.

He lived to be the despair of those modern men who, since youth, have been turned aside into a specialized activity, in which they think to become superior because they are confined to it. The variety of methods is invoked, and the quantity of details, and the continual addition of facts and theories; with the result that the patient observer, the meticulous accountant of existence, the individual who reduces himself, not without merit—if this word has any meaning!—to the minute habitudes of an instrument, is confused with the man for whom this labour is performed—the poet of the hypothesis, the builder with analytical materials. To the first, patience, monotonous direction, specialization, and all time. The absence of thought is his quality. But the other must circulate through barriers and partitions. His rôle is to overstep them. At this point I might suggest an analogy between specialization and the states of stupor due to prolonged sensation, which I mentioned some pages above. But the best argument consists in the observation that, nine times out of ten, every great improvement in field of endeavour is obtained by the introduction of methods and notions which were unforeseen. Since we have attributed such advances to the formation first of images, then of idioms, we cannot escape this consequence: that the number of such idioms possessed by any man has a singular bearing on his chances to find new ones. It would be easy to demonstrate that all the minds which have served as substance to whole generations of seekers and quibblers; all the intellects whose remains have nourished, for centuries on end, both human opinion and our weakness for being echoes, have been more or less universal. The names of Aristotle, Descartes, Leibnitz, Kant, Diderot are sufficient confirmation.

This leads us to another topic: the joys of *construction*. I will try to justify the preceding opinions by a few examples, and will attempt to show, in its application, the possibility and almost the necessity of a general interplay of thought. And I should like to point out that the particular results on which I shall touch would be difficult to obtain without our employing a number of apparently unrelated concepts.

The man who has never been seized—were it in a dream!—by a project which he is free to abandon, or by the adventure of a construction which is completed when others see that it has begun; who has never experienced either the fire of enthusiasm which utterly consumes a moment of himself, or the poison of conception, scruples, the coldness of interior objections, and this struggle between alternative ideas in which the stronger and more universal should triumph, even over habit, even over originality—the man who never, in the whiteness of his paper, has seen an image troubled by the possible and by regret for all the symbols which will not be chosen; nor has seen, in the limpid air, a building which does not exist—the man who is never haunted by the dizziness of a distant aim, the anxiety as to means, the foreknowledge of delays and despair, the planning of progressive phases, or the reasoning which is projected into the future to discover even those things which must not *then* be reasoned about—this man, however great his knowledge, will never know the riches, and the resources, and the broad spiritual domain, which are illuminated by the conscious fact of *constructing*. And the gods received their gift of *creating* from the human mind, because this mind, being periodic and abstract, can expand any of its conceptions to the point of their no longer being conceivable by the mind.

To construct is an act which exists between a project or determinate vision and the materials which one has chosen. For one order of things, which is initial, we substitute another, whatever may be the nature of the objects rearranged. They are stones, colours, words, concepts, men, etc.; their particular nature does not change the general conditions of that sort of music in which, at this point, the chosen material serves only as the timbre, if we pursue the metaphor. The wonder is that we feel, sometimes, that exactness and consistency exist in human constructions, in spite of their being composed of an agglomeration of apparently incompatible elements; it would seem that the mind which arranged these elements had known their secret affinities. But wonder passes all bounds when we perceive that the author, in the vast majority of cases, is incapable of describing, even to himself, the paths which he followed to reach this goal; and that he is master of a power whose nature he does not know. He can never assert in advance that he will be successful. By what process are the parts of an edifice, the elements of a drama, the factors in a victory, harmonized one with another? What series of obscure analyses is necessary to produce a work?

In similar cases it is the custom to explain everything by instinct, but the nature of instinct is itself too vague. And, moreover, the present example is one we should have to explain by instincts strictly personal and exceptional; in other words, by the contradictory notion of an "hereditary habit" which would be no more habitual than it was hereditary.

The act of construction, as soon as it arrives at some intelligible result, would suggest that a common measure of terms has been applied; but this element or principle has already been presupposed by the simple fact of our becoming conscious, and could possess only an abstract or imaginary existence. We cannot conceive of a whole composed of changes—a picture or an edifice of multiple qualities—except as the locus of the attributes of a single *matter* or *law*, whose hidden continuity we affirm in the very same instant that we recognize this edifice as a united whole, as the limited field of our investigation. Once more we encounter that psychical postulate of continuity which, in the domain of the mind, resembles the principle of inertia in mechanics. Only such purely abstract and purely differential combinations as those of mathematics can be constructed with the aid of fixed units; and it is to be noted that the relation of these to other possible constructions is the same as that of the regular portions of the world to those which are not regular.

A word exists in art which can describe all its modes and fantasies, and suppress, at a stroke, all the pretended difficulties involved in the opposition or resemblance between art and the "nature" which is never defined, and for good reason—that word is *ornament*. Let us recall, successively, the groups of curves or intersecting figures which cover the oldest known objects, and the profiles of vases or of temples; then the lozenges, volutes, ova and striæ of the ancients; the crystallizations and voluptuous walls of the Arabs; the skeletal symmetry of the Gothic; the fires and flowers on Japanese lacquer or bronze; and, in each of these epochs, the introduction of the likenesses of plants, animals, or men, the perfection of these resemblances: painting, sculpture. Let us consider speech and its primitive melody, the separation of words and music and the development of each: on the one hand the invention of verbs, of writing, the *figurative* complexity of phrases becoming possible, and the curious intervention of abstract words; on the other hand, the system of tones growing more supple, extending from the voice to the resonance of materials, being enriched by harmony, being varied by the use of different timbres. And finally, let us observe the parallel progress of the formations of thought: first through a sort of primitive psychic onamatopœia, then through elementary symmetries and contrasts, till it finally reaches the ideas of substances, metaphors, a stammering logic, formalism, entities, metaphysical beings. . . .

All this multiform activity can be regarded from the standpoint of ornament. The manifestations we have listed can be considered as finished portions of space or time. They contain different variations. Some of these are known and described objects, but their ordinary meaning and use are neglected, so that only their order and mutual relations are allowed to subsist. On this order and these mutual relations depends the effect. The effect is the aim of ornament, and thus the work of art assumes the character of a machine to impress a public; to arouse emotions and their corresponding images.

From this angle, the conception of ornament bears the same relation to all the arts that mathematics bears to all the sciences. Just as the physical notions of time, length, density, mass, etc., exist in mathematical computations merely as homo-

geneous quantities, and recover their individuality
only when the results are interpreted—so the objects which are chosen and arranged to secure an
effect are, as it were, detached from most of their
attributes, and only reassume them in this effect
—that is, in the unbiased mind of the spectator.
Hence, it is by a sort of abstraction that the work
of art is constructed; and this abstraction is more
or less energetic, more or less easy to define, according to whether the elements taken from reality are
more or less complex. Inversely, it is by a sort of
induction, by the production of mental images,
that any work of art is appreciated; and this production must equally be more or less energetic,
more or less *tiring,* according to whether it is
aroused by a simple moulding on an urn, or by
one of Pascal's broken phrases.

The painter arranges oily pigments on a plane,
and expresses himself by means of their thickness
and lines of separation, their blendings and clash-
ings. What the spectator sees is only a more or
less faithful image of flesh, gestures, or landscape,
as if he were looking through a window in the
museum. The picture is judged in the same spirit

as reality. Some observers are enamoured with the
face, and others complain of its ugliness; still others
are psychological and verbose; a few look only at
the hands, which they always call unfinished. The
fact is that the picture, in accordance with un-
spoken demands, must reproduce the physical and
natural conditions of our environment. Light
radiates and weight is felt, just as in the world of
reality; and, gradually, anatomy and perspective
take their place in the first rank of pictorial studies.
I believe, however, that the surest method of judg-
ing a picture is to recognize nothing at first; and
then, step by step, to make the series of inductions
which are demanded by the simultaneous presence
of coloured spots in a limited field; to rise from
metaphor to metaphor, from supposition to supposition; and so, finally, to attain to knowledge of
the subject—or sometimes merely to the consciousness of pleasure, which we did not always feel at
first.

No example I could give of the general attitude
toward painting would be more amusing than the
celebrity of the "smile of Mona Lisa," to which
the epithet of mysterious seems irrevocably fixed.
This wrinkle in her face has aroused the sort of

phraseology which justifies, in all literatures, the title of "Sensations" or "Impressions" of art. It is buried beneath a mass of words, and disappears among the myriad paragraphs which commence by calling it "troubling," and end by a generally vague description of a state of *soul*. It would justify less intoxicating studies. Leonardo made no use of inexact observations and arbitrary symbols, or Mona Lisa would never have been painted. A perpetual wisdom guided him.

In the background of the Last Supper, there are three windows. The one in the middle, which opens behind Jesus, is distinguished from the others by a cornice which is the arc of a circle. If we prolong this arc, we obtain a circumference whose centre is the Christ. All the great lines of the fresco converge at this point; the symmetry of the whole is relative to the centre, and to the long line of the table of the agape. The mystery, if one exists, is to know why we consider such combinations to be mysterious; and this, I fear, can be explained.

It is not from painting, however, that we shall choose our salient example of the communication between the different activities of thought. The horde of suggestions which rise from the painter's need to diversify and people a surface; the resemblance between the first attempts of this order and certain dispositions of nature; the evolution of visual sensibility—all these will be disregarded at this point, for fear of guiding the reader toward far too arid speculations. An art more vast; the ancestor, as it were, of painting, will serve our purpose better.

The word *construction*—which I purposely employed, so as to express the problem of human intervention in natural things more forcibly, and to direct the mind of the reader toward the logic of the subject by a material suggestion—now resumes its limited meaning. Architecture becomes our example.

The *monument* (which composes the City, which in turn is almost the whole of civilization) is such a complex entity that our understanding of it passes through several successive phases. First we grasp a changeable background which merges into the sky; then a rich texture of architectural motifs, infinitely varied by perspective; then something solid, bold, resistant, with certain animal

269

characteristics—organs, functions, members—then finally, a machine having gravity for its motive force, and guiding our thoughts from geometrical notions to dynamic considerations; even, perhaps, to the most tenuous speculations of molecular physics, of which science it suggests the theories and representative formations. It is by means of such a monument; or rather, by considering the imaginary scaffoldings which its architect must have conceived, in order to harmonize its conditions one with the other—its appropriateness with its stability, its proportions with its background, its form with its matter—and in order to make each of these conditions accord with itself, its millions of aspects with one another, its three dimensions with one another—that we are best able to reconstitute the clear intelligence of a Leonardo. He can amuse himself by imagining the future sensations of the man who will make a circuit of the building, draw near, look through a window, and what this stranger will see—by following the weight of the roofs as it is carried along walls and arches, till it finally reaches the foundation—by feeling the thwarted efforts of the beams, and the vibration of the winds which haunt them—by picturing the forms of the light which will play over tiles and cornices, and grow diffuse as it is caged in rooms where the sun goes dabbling on the floor. He will test and judge the pressure of the lintel on its supports, the opportunities of the arch, the difficulties of the vaults, the cascades of steps which will gush from beneath the portico, and all the power of invention which he has concentrated in a durable mass—embellished, defended, made liquid with windows; fashioned for our lives, to contain our works, to belch forth the smoke of our chimneys.

Generally, architecture is misunderstood. Our attitude varies, and we sometimes desire a stage-setting, sometimes a tenement house. However, if we refer to our concept of the City, we can realize the universality of this art; and by recalling the multiplicity of its aspects, we can appreciate its complex charm. That a building should be motionless is an exception; our pleasure arises from moving about it in such manner that we make the building move; we enjoy all the combinations of its members, which vary: the column turns, depths appear, galleries glide, a thousand visions rise from the monument, a thousand harmonies.

(Many a project for a church, never realized, is to be found in Leonardo's manuscripts. One of his drawings is generally taken for a St. Peter's; it makes us regret that of Michael Angelo. At the end of the Gothic period, and during the excavation of ancient temples, Leonardo found, between the two types, the great design of the Byzantines: a cupola rising above cupolas; domes topped with swelling domes that cluster about the highest dome of all. His work, however, shows a boldness and pure ornamentation which Justinian's architects never knew.)

The monument, that creature of stone, exists in space. What we call space is relative to the existence of whatever structures we may choose to conceive. Among these, the architectural structure interprets space, and leads to hypotheses on the nature of space, in a very particular manner; for it is an equilbrium of materials with respect to gravity, a visible static whole, and, at the same time, in each of its materials, another equilibrium—molecular, in this case, and imperfectly known. The man who designs a monument first imagines its weight, and then immediately penetrates into the obscure atomic realm. He is faced with the general

problem of structure: that is, to know what combinations are necessary in order to satisfy the conditions of resistance, elasticity, etc., required in a
given space. We can see the logical steps by which
the problem is widened, and how one passes from
the architectural domain, generally abandoned to
specialists, into the most profound theories of mechanics and of physics in general.

Thanks to the agility of the imagination, the
properties of an edifice and those inherent in a
given substance help to explain each other. Space,
as soon as we try to represent it in our minds, ceases
at once to be a void, and is peopled with a mass of
arbitrary constructions; or at least it can be replaced by juxtaposed forms, which we render as
small as necessary. However complex we may suppose an edifice to be, it will represent, when multiplied and proportionally diminished, the element of
a formation of space whose qualities will all depend
on this element. Hence, we are surrounded by and
move among an infinite quantity of structures.
Let us observe, for example, in how many different
fashions the space around us is occupied (in other
words, is formed, is conceivable) ; and let us try to
grasp the conditions implied by our perception of

various things with their particular qualities: a fabric, a mineral, a liquid, a cloud of smoke. We can gain a clear idea of these textures only by enlarging one of their particles, and by inserting, into this particle, a structure so organized that by simple multiplication it will form a substance having the same qualities as the substance under consideration. . . . By the aid of concepts like these, we can move continuously through the domains of the artist and the scientist, although their realms are apparently so distinct; and we can proceed from the most poetic, even from the most fantastic, construction to one which is tangible and ponderable. The problems of composition and those of analysis are reciprocal; and when our age abandoned its too simple concepts with regard to the constitution of matter, it gained a triumph no less *psychological* than that of abandoning similar concepts with regard to the formation of ideas. Dogmatic explanations of nature and transcendentalist reveries are disappearing at the same time; and the science of forming hypotheses, names, models, is being liberated from preconceived theories and the idol of simplicity.

I have just indicated, with a brevity for which the reader will either thank or excuse me, an evolution which I believe to be considerable. I could give no better example of the resulting state of mind than to quote from the writings of Leonardo himself. Of the sentence which follows, one might say that each of its terms has been so purified and complicated as to become a concept fundamental to our modern understanding of the world:

"The air," he says, "is filled with an infinite number of lines, straight and radiating, intercrossing and weaving together without ever coinciding; and they *represent* for every object the true FORM of their reason (of their explanation). *L'aria è piena d'infinite linee rette e radiose insieme intersegate e intessute senza occupazione l'una dell'altra rappresentano qualunque obietto la vera forma della lor cagione.*" (Manuscript A, Folio 2.)

This sentence seems to contain the first germ of the theory of light waves, especially when it is compared with other remarks which Leonardo made on the same subject.[10] It gives the skeleton, as it

10 See Manuscript A, *Siccome la pietra gittata nell'acqua* . . . etc.; also the curious and lively *Histoire des Sciences Mathématiques*, by G. Libri, and the *Essai sur les Ouvrages Mathématiques (de Léonard)*, by J-B. Venturi (Paris, *An* V—1797).

were, of a system of waves; all these lines would be
their direction of propagation. However, I do not
set much store by scientific prophecies of the sort;
they are always suspicious; far too many people
believe that the ancients discovered everything.
Besides, a theory is worth only as much as its logical
and experimental developments. And in this particular instance we possess only a few affirmations,
based intuitively on the observation of rays, as they
exist in waves of sound or water. The interest of
the quotation resides in its form, which gives us authentic light on a method—the very method I have
been discussing throughout this essay.

Leonardo's explanation does not *as yet* assume
the character of a measurement. It consists only
in the emission of an image, a concrete mental
relation between phenomena—let us say, to be exact—between the images of phenomena. It would
seem that he was aware of this sort of psychic ex-
perimentation; and I do believe that, for three centuries after his death, the method was ever recognized, though every one made use of it—necessarily.

I also believe—though perhaps it is going too far
—that the famous and secular question of ether
and vacuum can be related to our being conscious

or unconscious of this *imaginative logic*. Thus, an action at a distance is something which cannot be imagined. We can define it only by use of an abstraction. In our minds, only an abstraction *potest facere saltus*, can make a leap. Even Newton, who gave their analytic form to actions at a distance, realized that they were inadequate as explanations. But to rediscover Leonardo's method, as applied to physics, was an honour reserved for Faraday. After the glorious mathematical researches of Lagrange, d'Alembert, Laplace, Ampère, and many others, he introduced admirably bold conceptions which were literally only the prolongation, by his imagination, of observed phenomena; and his imagination was so remarkably lucid "that his ideas were capable of being expressed in the ordinary mathematical forms, and thus compared with those of the professed mathematicians." [11] The *regular combinations* formed by iron filings around the poles of a magnet were, in his mind, the models of the transmission of the former "actions at a distance." Like Leonardo, he *saw* systems of lines uniting all bodies, filling the whole

[11] Preface to the treatise on *Electricity and Magnetism*, by J. Clerk Maxwell.

of space; and in this way *explained* electrical phenomena and even gravity. For the purposes of the essay, we can regard such lines of space as those of least resistance to the understanding. Faraday was not a mathematician, but he differed from mathematicians only by the expression of his thought, by the absence of the symbols of analysis. "Faraday, in his mind's eye, saw lines of force traversing all space, where mathematicians saw centres of force attracting at a distance; Faraday saw a medium where they saw nothing but distance." [12] Beginning with Faraday, a new era opened for physical science; and when J. Clerk Maxwell had translated his master's ideas into the language of mathematics, scientific imaginations were filled with similar dominating visions. The study of the medium which he formed—the scene of electrical activity and intermolecular reactions—remains the principal occupation of modern physics. Inspired partly by the demand for greater and greater precision in representing the modes of energy, partly by the will to *see*, and partly by something which might be called the kinetic mania, hypotheses have appeared, or hypothetical constructions, which are

[12] J. Clerk Maxwell.

logically and psychologically of the greatest interest. For Lord Kelvin, to give one example, the
need of expressing the most subtle natural actions
by a mental connexion, and of carrying this connexion to the point where it can be realized in
matter, is so keen that he feels every explanation
should lead to a mechanical model. Such a mind
rejects the inert atom, the mere point imagined by
Boscovich and the physicists of the early nineteenth century; and in its place sets an extraordinarily complex mechanism, caught in a web of
ether, which itself becomes a very elaborate structure in order to satisfy the widely divergent conditions it must fulfil. A mind like his passes without effort from the architecture of crystals to that
of stone or iron; in our viaducts, in the symmetries
of beams and joists, he finds the symmetries of resistance which quartz and gypsum offer to com-
pression and cleavage—or, differently, to the passage of rays of light.

Such men appear to have had an intuition of the
methods which we indicated. We might even permit ourselves to extend these methods beyond the
limits of physical science; and we believe that it
would neither be absurd nor entirely impossible to

create a model of continuity from the intellectual operations of a Leonardo da Vinci, or from those of any other mind selected after analysis of the conditions to be fulfilled.

The artists and connoisseurs of art who have turned these pages in hope of finding some of the impressions to be gathered at the Louvre, in Florence, or in Milan, must excuse me for the present disappointment. Nevertheless, I do not believe that I have wandered too far from their favourite occupation, in spite of appearances. I believe, on the contrary, that I have touched on their central problem, that of composition. I shall doubtless astonish many by saying that difficulties relative to the effect of a work of art are generally approached and solved by means of words and notions which are not only extraordinarily obscure, but involve a thousand difficulties. More than one writer has passed a lifetime in changing his definition of *the beautiful*, or *life*, or *mystery*. However, ten minutes of simple attention to oneself should suffice to destroy these idols of the cave, and to realize the inconsistency of attaching an abstract noun, always empty, to an always personal, a strictly personal, vision. Most discouragements of artists are of the same nature, being founded on the impossibility of their *rendering*, by the methods of their art, an image which loses colour and withers, so they think, as soon as it is caught in a phrase, on a canvas, or in a certain key. In this case, a few moments of further intuition will make it unnecessary to admit that wishing to reproduce the fantasies of one's mind in that of another is a mere illusion. We might even say that this project is nearly incomprehensible.

What critics call a *realization*, or a successful rendering, is really a problem of efficiency, in which the particular meaning—the key—attributed by every author to his materials plays no part, but in which the only factors are the nature of these materials and the mentality of the public. Edgar Allan Poe—who, in a troubled century of literature, was the lightning of the confusion and the poetic storm; whose analysis sometimes ends, like that of Leonardo, in mysterious smiles—has clearly established his appeal to the reader on the basis of psychology and probable effects. From this angle, every combination of elements made to be perceived and judged depends on a few general laws, and on a particular adaptation defined in advance for that chosen category of minds to which the whole is specially addressed; and the work of art becomes a machine designed to arouse and combine the individual formations of these minds. This suggestion is quite opposite to the ordinary idea of the sublime, and I foresee the indignation it will arouse; but that very indignation will be a good proof of what I hold—without this essay's being in any respect a work of art.

I can see Leonardo da Vinci delving into mechanics, which he called the paradise of the science, with the same natural resources he devoted to the invention of pure and misty faces. And the same luminous territory that he peopled with the docile tribe of possible constructions, is the scene of those actions which, by losing their velocity, become distinct works. In all his studies his passions remained the same; and, on the last page of that slender notebook, scored with his ciphered writing and adventurous calculations, in which he gropes toward his favourite research, aviation, he exclaims—thundering against his imperfect labour, illuminating his patience and its obstacles by the apparition of

a supreme spiritual view, an obstinate certainty:
—"The great bird will take its first flight on the
back of its great swan, and filling the universe with
stupor, filling all writings with its renown, and
eternal glory to the nest where it was born! *Pig-
lierà il primo volo il grande uccello sopra del dosso
del suo magno cecero e empiendo l'universo di
stupore, empiendo di sua fama tutte le scritture e
gloria eterna al nido dove nacque.*"

THE END

283

DATE DUE			

Valéry   222471